WHO TAKES THIS
CHILD?

Also by Allan Dare Pearce

Paris in April

WHO TAKES THIS
CHILD?

A Parents' Guide
to Child Protection in Canada

ALLAN DARE PEARCE

iUniverse LLC
Bloomington

WHO TAKES THIS CHILD?
A Parents' Guide to Child Protection in Canada

The Law Society of Upper Canada allows me to practice law as a barrister and solicitor in the Province of Ontario. Previously, I practised law in the Northwest Territories for a brief period. Protection matters across the country in Canada remain somewhat similar in nature, possessing ancestry and many features in common, but they still vary from jurisdiction to jurisdiction, sometimes in substantive ways. Parents involved in protection cases should seek out and retain experienced counsel to represent them. This book is not intended to be legal advice, nor should it be construed as such but merely as some reflections on common protection issues in Canada. Notwithstanding anything outlined above or anything that follows, the best piece of advice I can impart to a parent involved in a protection proceeding remains this: you need a lawyer in your corner. If matters have progressed to the litigation stage, you definitely need a lawyer to help you assess the protection issues and render advice on how to address them, as well as to assist you with the interim issues prior to trial, and, finally, at trial. If you choose not to get a lawyer, here is my advice: take your kids aside, one at a time, and kiss them good-bye.

iUniverse books may be ordered through booksellers or by contacting:

iUniverse LLC
1663 Liberty Drive
Bloomington, IN 47403
www.iuniverse.com
1-800-Authors (1-800-288-4677)

ISBN: 978-1-4917-0092-1 (sc)
ISBN: 978-1-4917-0093-8 (ebk)

Library of Congress Control Number: 2013914014

Printed in the United States of America

iUniverse rev. date: 08/08/2013

Contents

For Mary Anne,
my partner since our days in law school.

Introduction

No provincial government commissioned this report; no federal government department sought me out, dumped money on me pleading for my two cents on this topic. The proceeds from this book will not find their way into charitable matters and you receive no deductible expense for Revenue Canada. I consulted no ivory tower experts, collected no tangible evidence, kept no prisoners, just drilled down my experiences and observations from 35-plus years in practice, doing mostly child protection work. Few books discuss child protection matters in Canada and none direct their comments toward parents. This is not a book about Child Protection law but rather about what happens in a protection case in Canada.

For more than thirty years I have counselled and represented parents in their battles with the child protection authorities, preparing pleadings, arguing motions and conducting trials.

I offer one personal war story about child protection to demonstrate how easy it is to misread a protection situation. Years ago, working for the government of the Northwest Territories, I acted for the government in a protection matter, my one and only effort on the prosecution side of the fence. On the shores of the Arctic Ocean squats the village of Tuktoyaktuk, "Tuk" to the several hundred locals. The lawyers, judge and witnesses, with court reporter in tow, all flew into Tuk in the same Twin Otter plane to conduct this particular protection trial. The ocean shores description raised my suspicion, as the lonely place just appeared to be ice and snow stretching on forever, wrapping around a cluster of 40 or 50 buildings and the town hall.

During the trial, even though relatively inexperienced, I cross-examined the mother on the witness stand with brilliance, and she conceded point after damaging point. I sweetly established the government's case—very sweetly indeed. I remember thinking, *I can embrace this sort of legal life, taking kids away from bad parents; not a bad life at all.* My cross-examination seemed to inflame the judge against the mother as well, and he lit into her with unrestrained vigour, suggesting that her children would fare better in care, visibly shaking the woman. My case tumbled in well on every point—my first major victory, I assumed, pushing me toward an outstanding career as a litigator, a Clarence Darrow of the north, perhaps. When the judge rendered his decision, he seized the opportunity to berate the mother again. And then, to my astonishment, after yelling at her at great length, he gave the kids back to her. *He gave the kids back to her!* During a trial that lasted several hours, I had apparently been absent—possibly out searching for the rumoured ocean. Perhaps I'd misread the evidence, perhaps misunderstood the judge, or maybe I inhabited a parallel universe where everything turned reverse or upside down. What the hell?

After the trial we dumped our gear back into the same Otter to return home to Yellowknife. The judge claimed the front seat beside the pilot, and we two lawyers parked ourselves behind him. Once airborne, the judge pulled out a bottle of hard liquor (those were relaxed times) and poured a few inches into a paper cup for each of us, while he explained his logic.

"If I'm going to take the kids," he said, "I flail away at the Agency or Society to give the parent some small satisfaction; if I am going to give back the kids, I beat up the parent, scare the crap out of her so she knows she'd better step up her parenting skills."

Two morals pop out of this story. First, keep your eye on the ball—look at what judges do rather than what they say; they all started out life as lawyers, so they can pound words into whatever suits their immediate purpose. At the end of the day, look at who actually gets the kid. But on a different level, examine what happened in this case. Truth be told, lawyers are not overly concerned with the pursuit of truth; they must not mislead the court, but they put their client's position to the court as zealously as they can, and in so doing they often fail to assess the worth of their client's position on any meaningful level. This remains the first role of the lawyer in the court process—to argue for your client, and I, with the other counsel in Tuktoyaktuk, fulfilled that function with vigour, arguing up a damn storm. The judge, however, set himself only one task—he merely did the right thing for the child: identifying the risk, assessing the risk and satisfying himself on the best way to deal with that risk.

To recap, we lawyers argued with gusto, generally providing great theatre for the Inuit audience on that particular day. But the lawyers stood as mostly irrelevant to the process.

And this is the way a protection matter usually plays out: the judge cooks up an intuitive decision about the child based upon her reading of the testimony and evidence, lawyers notwithstanding.

Do lawyers serve a purpose in the protection system? The most productive uses of a lawyer in a protection matter: to help the client present a reasonable plan to address the protection concerns and to assist the client in putting that plan directly to the court. Unfortunately, given the nature of many clients, with their limitations, their incendiary natures and worsening family dynamics, the lawyer's primary role will often be to simply unleash the arguing. In such a case, your lawyer may just as well argue statute law, incomprehensible regulations, weird alien theories or that nifty case she discovered from the High Court of Nepal, the one that dealt with the abused tiger cubs. But very few arguments will sway a judge from her intuitive feeling about the risk to a child in a protection case.

Chapter 1

The System That Protects Children

The Society, or the Agency, or Children's Aid Society (CAS), or whatever name they use in your jurisdiction—perhaps the Orwellian "Director," in the case of Alberta—enjoys enormous power that many lay people never twig to. If "the Agency" harbours serious concerns about your child, founded or unfounded, a worker simply attends your home, with police assistance, and removes the child. The child remains in the care of the Agency until the Agency or a judge relents, concluding the concerns false or the perceived risk to the child adequately addressed, resulting in the child returning to you—albeit somewhat traumatized by the experience.

The Agency is all-powerful and aggressive, and the court system and judges are extremely reluctant to rein them in. Even with an experienced and diligent lawyer in your corner, you face an uphill battle to take away the protection concerns raised by the Agency. In the main, the challenge for the court is whether your child needs protection or intervention—essentially, whether your child is in danger, at risk, or perhaps facing a threat from you. When a parent or a person caring for a child inflicts injury to that child—or even fails to protect a child from physical or emotional harm (yes, emotional harm: "Oh my God, you got *what* for Christmas?")—the court may conclude that the child needs protection, even when the parent bears no blame. The concept of harm to a child encompasses an active duty to protect a child ("Get away from the highway, kid"). Failure to supervise or watch over the child—for instance, failure to protect the child from sexual molestation or exploitation—could also result in a protection finding or intervention. In most jurisdictions, the

1

concept of protecting a child extends to situations in which a reasonable person *should have known* or *was likely to know* about risk to a child. The concept includes a failure to seek out medical treatment for a child on a timely basis. A protection issue surfaces when a child is abnormally depressed, anxious, withdrawn or exhibiting self-destructive, aggressive or delayed development—if the parent ignores or fails to recognize these conditions. In brief, virtually every risk to a child, if not addressed by the parent, raises a protection issue. And the term *parent* includes anyone entrusted with care of the child.

The judge makes an intuitive decision about whether your child is at risk from you or the situation, but if you wish to quantify that risk in order to address it or to predict the outcome, a useful checklist is contained in the various protection provisions in your jurisdiction. (See the appendix at the end of this book for a list of these provisions in the various territories or provinces.) The provisions are similar across the country, but, as noted, are not applied in any formalistic fashion at trial; the judge in front of you will not be reviewing those provisions with a magnifying glass before he or she makes a decision. However, these issues will raise a red flag with the worker, and the issues will come into play in any protection proceeding.

Most complaints filed with the Agency are resolved without court process, by the Agency worker and his or her supervisor bringing a commonsense evaluation to the situation. Very few of the average worker's files turn into court battles.

The ever-present reality facing the parent

A child in care suffers damage: perhaps not physical damage—though on occasion there is physical damage—but certainly emotional damage, which may or may not (usually *not*) be addressed during care. Children apprehended at birth and adopted out may avoid this fate, but for all other children in care, you should assume they have been damaged. This fact alone should furnish any reasonable parent with extreme anxiety, if not apoplexy, before they engage in litigation with the Agency. The Agency has no golden palace with princes and princesses to care for your child, only human beings prepared to care for the child in return for money, and usually *only* in return for money. I have cross-examined foster parents in the past who challenge Mother Theresa in the area of good intentions, and follow through, but they are in the minority, albeit a blessed minority. However well intentioned most foster parents may be, a decent family structure remains the preferred setting to care for a child. Therefore, as lawyers say, *govern yourself accordingly* before you push the Agency into the legal arena.

There is no "Orlando option"

People outside the system often assume that when the Agency "acquires" a child, the young soul pops onto a first-class voyage to Orlando, furnished with a lifetime pass to Disney World and residence at a five-star hotel where Mary Poppins visits daily to entertain. Sadly, no "Orlando option" exists for kids in care. Kids in long-term care suffer abrupt upheaval followed by a trainload of trauma as they bounce from foster home to foster home, connecting with few people and arriving finally at the dumping ground. "Good luck, child," the Agency says. "We've warehoused you until you reach the age of 16—or maybe 18 or 19—and now we are dropping you into an adult world as a fissured soul. Don't bother to write. Don't come home for Christmas." *Plop.*

The Agency is directly or indirectly an arm of a provincial or territorial government—the same government that levies taxes, collects taxes, overshoots budget projections, and steps in deep doo-doo on a regular basis. Leaving aside the cases involving obvious abuse, which usually present as a no-brainer, the argument that the Canada Post and Revenue Canada display far more adeptness at discharging their duties than child welfare agencies do is tenable. This is so for obvious reasons. Assessing risk to a child involves myriad judgment calls, perhaps the following:

- assessing emotional injury to a child
- assessing the conduct of parents
- assessing the capabilities of parents

- deciding if drugs or alcohol pose a problem
- assessing the needs of the child
- reviewing possible alternative placements for the child
- searching for other remedies short of apprehending children
- the potential effect of the situation and of the above issues on the child in question.

These issues would test the wisdom of King Solomon. The presence of young, sometimes inexperienced, workers who are occasionally prone to overreaction complicates the subject even further. Perhaps the duty to rescue children in peril seems glamorous while students repose in classrooms pursuing that Master of Social Welfare (MSW) degree, but prying into people's homes and lives and sorting through the emotional garbage of families to accurately assess risk to a child qualifies as a damn crappy job. The burnout rate of workers is ferocious because of the stress it entails.

Cookies and tea

The vanguard workers, the shock troops of the Agency, usually consist of young sometimes inexperienced line workers charged with seeking out children who are in need of protection.

A word about the typical child welfare worker: this soul is normally a young woman with a university degree in social work or something similar. She chose social work as her vocation out of a genuine desire to help people. This young woman, often much younger than the parents she visits, did not grow up in the bad part of town or in a ghetto. Parental conflict in her youth probably involved abrupt channel changes by her mother in the middle of a New Year's Day football game. She theoretically understands how to change a diaper, and she can spot a high temperature, but she has never had to cool a child down in a tepid bath in the middle of the night to fight a raging fever. During her typical day, she faces big-time attitude from most of the parents she visits. No one invites her in for cookies and tea. For Agency parents, she is the person taking notes and preparing the court case against them, a person they view with apprehension at the best of times. However, of all the people they should invite in for tea and cookies, she may actually rank at the head of the list. Every worker reports to a supervisor, who somewhat balances out the worker's inexperience, but supervisors often carry additional baggage that affects the situation—namely, "the curse of child-protection work."

The curse of child-protection work

This curse probably visits this supervisor in her dreams or in moments when she reflects on her career choices. As a seasoned veteran supervisor, she has participated in a case that turned ugly, a case in which serious harm came to a child at the hands of parents. This curse affects everyone in the system, and it scars many workers and judges deeply. This curse is the reason why the system is inherently biased against parents. *Repeat: the system is inherently biased against parents.*

No judge gets up in the morning, looks in the mirror, and says, "Well, today I'm going to screw up someone's life." (Although to be perfectly honest, I never felt this way when one of them was yelling at me.) Nevertheless, the longer a judge hears messy child-protection cases, the greater are the chances of him or her committing an error. Like the worker's supervisor, the judge has misread a parent or a situation at some point and returned a child to parents who presented themselves well in court but who managed to keep the actual risk to the child a secret. A tragedy ensued. Perhaps a child was seriously burnt, beaten, maimed, or even died in the care of these parents. After that incident, that judge thinks, "Don't natter on to me about *burdens of proof* or *evidentiary issues*; don't spout on about *parental rights*; don't yap off about the *injustice of the system*—just prove to me, each and every dad and mom in my courtroom, just guarantee me that such a tragedy will never visit my courtroom again." That judge lives with the fact that he or she returned a child to a home where that child suffered grievous harm. The judge's intuitive decision turned out poorly, perhaps tragically. And this is the curse that haunts his or her courtroom forever, and this same curse permeates the system and precludes, delays, or inhibits the return of a child to good-and-proper parents.

What sort of duty do we implicitly impose upon our judges in the child-protection system? A baseball player who consistently hammers a base hit every third time at bat invariably pops into the Hall of Fame. But a sitting justice who succeeds in bringing justice 99 times out of 100, but the hundredth time involves the death of child, wins no awards from the local newspaper. The press, notable experts at back-seat driving, will pillory that justice unmercifully. The outcome in that one case will haunt his or her decisions in the years to come, whether intentionally or not. If a judge makes a mistake in a child-protection case, the consequence to a child can be horrendous. Of course, on the flip side, when the judge weighs the available options in any given case, even the most incompetent of societies usually—*but not always*—manages to keep the child in their care alive. If a judge makes a mistake and returns the child to incompetent parents, the tragedy hangs around his or her neck. If the same child dies in the care of the Agency, the rope is deflected from the judge and encircles the Agency's neck, so the risk is lower for the judge, or so some think. When we talk about the burden of proof in a child-protection case, the curse must be factored in, and this unknown component cannot be quantified by reading case law or statutes alone. It remains a haunting factor nonetheless.

Warning to parents: the Agency produces psychotics

Thousands of children plummet into the Agency's care, courtesy of court orders, every year. A few turn out extremely well, especially those who are adopted young, but others *don't* turn out so well. The Agency produces kids with a criminal bent—kids who disappear, kids damned with suicidal thoughts, kids who actually commit suicide—and of course, the Agency spawns more than its fair share of psychotics. No firm, verifiable figures exist about these things; many suspect that publishing accurate statistics on these issues would cast the entire system into question and generate pitchfork parades (rather than the occasional benign public inquiry after a few "routine" deaths during care). A possible recipe for producing a psychotic child might be as follows: take one child from a dysfunctional family, drop this kid into a foster home—not evil folks, but people who decide later, for their own reasons, not to be foster parents—and stir this child about, blending the child from foster home to foster home and perhaps tossing him or her into the occasional group home. Eventually the child develops reattachment issues or even spills out of the system as another protection-produced psychotic. As already noted, no Orlando option exists—so intelligent parents will keep their child from going into care if humanly possible! Not every child in care turns into a protection-produced psychotic, but few children thrive in care. Some do, but most—I repeat, *most*—don't. A child going into long-term care suffers trauma: sometimes severe, sometimes everlasting and sometimes devastating.

An easy fix

Is there a simple solution to saving your child from this pain and suffering? Yes, there is. Just suck it up and do what the Agency wants. Take the parenting course, dump that abusive spouse, give up alcohol, abandon drugs, submit to substance testing or clean the damned house. My observation from 30-plus years in this business is that children in care, especially long-term care, usually do not fare well. I repeat: children in care *usually*—not just *sometimes*—do not fare well.

The magic mouth

The first line of defence against the Agency is the mouth of the parent. God or circumstance furnishes most Agency clients with big-time attitude. Each and every parent on earth knows that his or her parenting skills exceed those of others, that he or she is actually an expert on child-raising. Accordingly, no parent accepts well the suggestion that they cannot care for their child properly—especially when the proposal comes from a young worker, perhaps fresh out of college, whose practical experience with children consists of babysitting the next-door neighbour's kid during his or her high-school years. But if you jump in and confront a worker, this will colour the case dramatically. Before you respond to the initial contact from a worker, pause and reflect. Properly motivated parents use their mouths to explain and to give the worker a comfort level about the care of these children. Criticism of the worker may be warranted, but the parent should consider the possibility that voicing these thoughts may not serve the children well. Children often pay stiff penalties for parents who lose control. Workers are allowed a great deal of discretion, and you should seek to have that discretion used on your behalf rather than against you. Much of the evidence of the Agency comes from this worker and the notes he or she takes. Build bridges, not walls; this will help your lawyer and neutralize or eliminate bad comments going into the Agency file.

When to bar the door

People with no previous history with the Agency often appear at my office and indicate that the Agency wants to meet with them. The question they put to me is, "Do I have to let them in?" Agency workers in most jurisdictions possess no right to enter your home without a warrant, but they can usually obtain a warrant without much effort and without your input into the process. Police officers possess wider statutory authority and are authorized to enter homes if they have reasonable grounds to suspect certain offences. But generally, the parent may assume that if the worker had serious concerns about the child, he or she would already have obtained a warrant *ex parte* (i.e., without your presence or input). Nevertheless, a confrontation at the door of his or her residence normally does not serve a parent well.

If the worker possesses no warrant, politely declining to admit him or her until you consult a lawyer remains within the bounds of acceptable behaviour, but it is not necessarily prudent. The law imposes stringent statutory duties upon the Agency to investigate every allegation, even when the allegations show little merit at face value. They must investigate these claims, and the parent meeting with the worker may resolve the matter with minimal intrusion. If the worker possessed serious concerns based upon reliable information about risk to the children, statutory obligations would have kicked in, and the children would have been apprehended—with or without warrant—and the matter plopped into court. A polite enquiry from a worker may telegraph the message that any perceived problems remain solvable and can be addressed at this point without court intervention, so a prudent parent might bite his or her tongue and invite the worker in. "May I offer you some cookies and tea?"

When deciding whether you should allow the worker into your home or bar the door, you might consider the following:

1. What sort of alleged behaviour is the worker talking about? You must possess some idea of what is driving this request. For a small problem or one that is easily remedied, you may safely bar the door. For a more serious risk, be assured that the Agency will pursue the matter, possibly with vigour.
2. Do the child's teachers indicate any problems with the child?
3. Has the child been acting out at home?
4. Have the police called the parents about any problems?
5. Do you possess any concerns about sexual or physical abuse? Have any relatives or friends been charged with possessing child porn, sex offences, or offences concerning young children?
6. How much do you drink? (You may substitute *smoke dope* or *do drugs* for the word *drink* and ask the question again.)
7. Is there serious parental conflict in the home?
8. Is your home clean and tidy? Has the Agency taken or tried to take pictures of the home?
9. How well are your children dressed?
10. Have you been getting feedback from the school about missing lunches? How are the children doing in school generally?

11. Do the teachers think your children are clean and well cared for? Has there been any unexplained drop in marks or change in their behaviour at school?
12. Are there any behaviour problems at daycare?
13. If the children have serious behavioural or medical problems, are professionals involved with the family? Do those professionals indicate that you are pursuing proper treatment programs?

Parents' rights

Teachers and school officials are a primary source of referrals to the Agency. A question often posed to lawyers concerns parents' rights. The issue arises when Agency workers show up at the school and jerk the children out of class to quiz them. The issue varies in different jurisdictions, but the central legal issues are outlined below.

As noted, the purpose of child-protection legislation remains the safeguarding of *the children*. Statutes or ordinances may give voice to saving the family or acknowledging parents' rights or other tangential issues, but the primary focus in every jurisdiction remains keeping the child safe, by apprehending or intervening in appropriate circumstances. The primary responsibility for this risk assessment falls on the Agency. In Canada, the argument that workers should not be allowed to question children at school rests primarily in the provisions of The Charter of Rights and Freedoms.

Section 7 of the Charter provides for the "right to life, liberty and the right not to be deprived thereof except in accordance with the principles of fundamental justice."

Section 9 provides: "Everyone has the right not to be arbitrarily detained or imprisoned."

Section 10 provides: "Everyone has the right on arrest or detention (a) to be informed promptly of the reason therefore; (b) to retain and instruct counsel without delay and to be informed of that right and (c) to have the validity of the detention determined by way of habeas corpus and to be released if the detention is not lawful."

The suggestion that, pursuant to the Charter, courts should place parental rights over child-protection concerns has yet to be squarely addressed in a higher court. In brief, there appears to exist no higher-court decision that holds or suggests that an Agency worker, by pulling your child out of class at the school and quizzing him or her, is violating these provisions of the Charter or, if the worker is, that these violations are not a "reasonable" limitation on Charter rights. The justices of provincial and territorial courts view the protection of children—not parental rights—as their primary, indeed sole, focus. At present, the right of a worker to talk to the child at school exists in practice throughout the country, and courts have shown little inclination to rein them in. As a matter of practice, the workers want to speak to the child away from parental influence, and this remains the logical forum for them to do so. Even though a child may be stigmatized by being pulled from class to be questioned by a protection worker, the above still applies. Until a higher court says it is not allowed, workers will continue to interview children at school.

So the question remains: when do you let the worker in the door and when do you bar it? If medical or behavioural problems plague your children and professionals are treating them for those problems, advising the worker of the name of the professionals involved and indicating a willingness to sign releases for those professionals should satisfy the worker. Blemish-free families may reject overtures from the Agency, but if the worker possesses any concerns, he or she will make the rounds, speaking to schoolteachers, neighbours, and perhaps even to the children. If the allegations concern parental misconduct, you need to address your issues before the Agency becomes a fixture in your life. But once again, reasonable parents do *not* engage in litigation against the Agency because of the probable adverse consequences to their children. If you reject Agency overtures, you can expect them to follow up. Investigating allegations sits as their primary function. They do it routinely, not necessarily out of any personal bias against any particular parent but seeking a comfort level with regard to the care of the children. Giving a comfort level to the worker usually plays out easier than the alternative—traipsing into court to do battle with the Agency.

Disclaimer

Despite the central premise that reasonable parents co-operate with the Agency or the sake of the children, cases proceed to court on regular and frequent basis. While strategies and tactics often unfold in similar fashion from jurisdiction to jurisdiction, remember that this book is not a substitute for legal advice. In any serious battle with the Society, parents should obtain the services of an experienced lawyer.

The best idiot lawyer money can't buy

Judges use a name for people who represent themselves in a protection matter. That name is—or ought to be—"idiot." Of course they don't say that out loud for fear of offending human-rights legislation, but that's probably what passes through their minds every time a self-represented person says the wrong thing and moves his or her child closer to becoming a permanent ward of the state.

The Supreme Court of Canada ruled that parents with financial need are entitled to have the government pay for their legal representation in a battle with the Agency over children. So if you meet the financial criteria, the provincial or territorial Legal Aid plan pays for your lawyer or provides one for you. If you do battle in court with the Agency, you will need a lawyer on your side. A lawyer knows what the court looks for, assesses the protection risk, and guides you in addressing the risk. But you also need someone who can provide a reality check on your position. In short, you need a lawyer, someone to put your case to the court in the best possible way; you need a lawyer. Try not to let this thought depress you overly.

How to choose a lawyer

There may not be enough lawyers in any given area who accept child-protection cases. The reasons vary, but child-protection cases often turn messy, becoming difficult, time-consuming and not always profitable. But more to the point, the perception exists that people in litigation with the Agency qualify automatically as bad parents or, worse, as child abusers. Reasonable people, people who believe a person involved with the criminal law system remains innocent until proven guilty, often discard similar feelings about people facing protection proceedings; this feeling exists among the legal community as well. If you live in an area where no lawyers are currently accepting child-protection cases, the concept of choosing a lawyer may, in fact, be academic. You may well have to settle for any lawyer who is willing to take your case. If you have tried and cannot obtain legal representation, you should contact the provincial or territorial law society, and failing that, the local bar association.

Having noted the above, the standard questions that you should put to a lawyer remain consistent with choosing a lawyer in other areas of the law. You will need to know: How much do they charge? What experience do they have in this type of case? What are the potential outcomes in this case? Can they give advice on the steps and procedures facing a parent? What can parents do to improve their position? What are the timelines in this case? Other questions on a practical level include: Does a parent receive copies of all documents and correspondence? Does the lawyer return phone calls? (Regardless of his or her response to this question, the actual answer is that they usually don't.)

By way of consolation, if the only available lawyer appears somewhat young, or perhaps has been called to the bar recently, child-protection cases have stringent timelines, and lawyers in this area of practice often gain experience somewhat faster than those in other areas of the law. Compared to other types of legal cases, a much higher percentage of cases in child protection do not get resolved, and they do involve contested litigation. As a result, that fresh-faced lawyer in front of you, the one who appears to be 12 years old, may actually have conducted more trials or extended litigation and be more experienced than someone who has worked a comparable period in another area of the law.

What your lawyer should do for you

1. Initially, your lawyer should assess your case, outline the options to you and indicate what the probable result will be. In protection cases, your lawyer should provide you with a reality check about your position. If you acknowledge this input and respond to it, your case will proceed faster.

2. Your lawyer should outline the procedure involved and provide rough timelines.

3. Your lawyer, or a properly instructed agent, should be with you at every court appearance. If you are like most parents seeking the return of a child in a protection matter, you will attend every court appearance. But you should not expect your lawyer to argue vociferously at every appearance. Specific purposes are attached to each court appearance; many deal with housekeeping chores, getting dates for argument or confirming consent matters or conferences between the parties. While you will ardently desire the injustice of your situation to be highlighted at each and every court appearance, with mounds of argument and wide-ranging submissions, judges usually have a full docket of cases in front of them, and they expect every lawyer to know the purpose of each court date and to deal with it in appropriate fashion. *Dang!*

4. Your lawyer should file comprehensive material on your behalf outlining your position to the court, as well as filings at the pleading stage for motions and for conferences. Nonetheless, you bear the ultimately responsible for ensuring that any document you sign is absolutely accurate. Review every document your lawyer presents for signature, and insist that it be true in every respect. Accuracy counts. Never leave the office without a copy of any document you've signed. But also listen to what is going on in court—and yes, unless your lawyer indicates otherwise, you should attend every court appearance. Judges routinely note

which parties are present in court. But sit back and listen. As a rule of thumb, competent lawyers file court material on a timely basis, without having to ask the court for extensions of time. If your lawyer is continually requesting extensions of time, it may serve as a red flag to you.

5.   Your lawyer or an assistant should respond to all phone calls from you. If you have a valid question or concern, leave it with the assistant one day and call back for an answer the following day. Most assistants have a good grasp of the process, and you should develop a relationship with them; they can answer almost all of your questions, except perhaps the most important one—Is your child going to be returned to you?

6.   Conscientious lawyers provide copies of all documents and correspondence to their clients, and prudent parents retain this material. Prudent parents also communicate clearly to their lawyers that receiving this material remains a priority for them. For self-represented people, the courthouse provides copies on request of any documents you do not possess.

7.   The government funds the great majority of child-protection cases—both sides, usually. However, if you are funding a lawsuit privately, you should obtain an estimate of the cost and an outline of any parameters affecting cost, including an estimated cost if the matter proceeds to trial. Press your lawyer for an hourly rate and the hourly rate of anyone else who may bill against your file. Question your counsel about what factors could increase your cost, and enquire about the cost of proposals recommended to advance your case in court. And—oh, yes—ask him or her to assess your case. Is your child going to be returned to you?

Chapter 2

The Radar Screen:
How the Agency Gets Involved

Several typical situations will bring parents into focus on the Agency's radar screen, and most of them suggest specific approaches to the lawyer representing you. No such list can be exhaustive, and the nature of the risk and of the "sighting" obviously will dictate the approach your lawyer recommends in preparing your defence strategy.

Radar sighting #1: The pregnant wife tests positive

The drug situations outlined below exist with more and more frequency—frightening frequency, in fact. These situations were virtually unknown when the Law Society of Upper Canada admitted me to the bar. This detection occurs when a pregnant mother attends the hospital and she tests positive for illegal drugs, whether for cannabis, or cocaine or morphine, or some other recreational drug. Hospital staff, rascals that they are, advise the Agency. A loud and persistent alarm bell signals a protection issue to the worker. *Bong*! If the positive test relates to a heavy-duty drug, the worker pursues the matter vigorously; an apprehension when the child is born now becomes a distinct possibility, even a probability. From this point, the attitude and actions of the parents become critical if they wish to avoid litigation. They will need an accurate and honest reality check forthwith and an immediate plan put in place on a timely basis. The worst-case scenario is that the Agency apprehends the child at birth. But if the mother, and perhaps her partner, submit to regular follicle testing and line up some counselling, the Agency may simply monitor the birth. To reemphasize: these circumstances require prompt and prudent action on the part of the parents. Nonetheless, a poor track record—say perhaps criminal conduct or previous drug involvement or big-time "attitude"—will likely to result in very aggressive action by the Agency.

Radar sighting #2: The child born with drugs in its system

Once again, the Agency will be alerted, and unless you resolve the matter along the above lines, the child will leave the hospital in the care of the Agency rather than in yours.

Radar sighting # 3: The child born with injuries consistent with abuse

Children are occasionally born with injuries consistent with abuse of the mother during pregnancy. Some injuries to a newborn may raise the possibility that the mother was assaulted during the pregnancy, presumably by an abusive spouse. Unlike the issue of drugs, no litmus test exists to prove or disprove these allegations. Allegations usually are based on expert medical opinion, opinions often sought in nearby medical centres, so the parents may face the expense of travelling to this centre as well as facing the normal trauma associated with apprehension of their child. Even more than in other protection cases, parents need experienced counsel to succeed in these situations. Collateral evidence, matters such as conditions in the home, plans of care or family dynamics often become secondary in importance. When the Agency's concern focuses on a spouse they suspect of abuse, the mother often must choose between the child and the spouse.

Radar sighting #4: The child with injuries in the emergency room

Emergency-room staff routinely consider the possibility of child abuse. While active children often break bones, other bruises on the child may appear consistent with abuse. Parents' reactions to staff or any inappropriate conduct in these situations often forms part of the Agency's case. Staff normally err on the side of caution and advise the Agency of suspicious injuries. In such cases, an existing relationship with a local family medical practitioner can help your situation. Reports from a family doctor confirming regular doctor's appointments for the child weigh in your favour or could even be a trump card. Doctors routinely note cuts and bruises, and the absence of such notations during previous regular visits to the family's health-care provider will work in your favour. If the child's injuries resulted from an accident, the sort of scrapes and bruises most kids suffer from time to time, collect the names of witnesses. Although a simple broken bone may not generate apprehension, it may generate a phone call by the worker to the child's teacher or to a neighbour.

The current drug culture gives rein to a more complicated approach when a child plunks into a hospital and the doctors or technicians on call discover that this child has ingested illegal substances, perhaps in large quantities. A word of caution in all of these situations: the legal doctrine of *res ipsa loquitur* ("the facts speak for themselves") applies, and you may not rely on the Agency's inability to prove fault. If the matter proceeds to court, you must present a reasonable or believable explanation for the harm. And, of course, when a child ingests illegal substances, any explanation poses as challenging at the best of times.

Radar sighting #5: The mother who has previously lost children to the Agency

It's a scene from hell: the pregnant woman in front of me, weeping, confesses to losing previous kids to the Agency. "What can I do to keep this one?" she asks. She pleads bad companions or faded addictions or sometimes just immaturity as the reason for the apprehension, and a few seconds later she outlines the major changes to her life. She has found God; she has found a good man; she has dumped a bad one; she has graduated from drug-addiction school or embraced Drunkards Anonymous; on one notable occasion, the reason was a fortuitous lightning strike. "What will happen when I give birth?" she asks. *There might be pain*, I want to say, but I suspect she seeks a profounder answer. In point of fact, Agency workers routinely keep problem parents on their radar screen and notify area hospitals about these people if they note a telltale bump. Agency staff assume that people who run, including pregnant women, run to familiar places rather than exotic ones, and a reading of any Agency file discloses backgrounds and ties, including the mother's birthplace, perhaps the birthplace of her spouse, or places that either resided in previously. Cooperation between different societies is always a given. If the woman disappears from the radar screen of one agency, other societies receive a prompt heads-up. For the woman who steps forward in this situation, ready to face the music and prepared to fight for this child, a good plan of care, supporting professionals, and a stable, informed, properly anchored support system remain key to winning over the Agency, or a judge, and early notification to the Society of the pregnancy is the place to start. The mom-to-be who declines to face the problem head-on courts disaster.

Radar sighting #6: The first fight when police are called

Police departments notify the Agency about any altercation between parents where children are present. Perhaps the children are huddled upstairs out of hearing, but no matter. The Agency's mandate includes intervening to protect children exposed to parental conflict, so following this initial contact, the Agency's weapons target you. The bull's eye is clearly painted on your back.

At the first involvement of the Agency in this sort of situation, you can assume that the criminal records of all parties are pulled and reviewed. Does the father have a long history of abusing spouses, or maybe just the occasional violent confrontation, or some previous convictions for assault? If so, the target on your back now glows or maybe flashes: *Shoot me, shoot me.* The radar switches on full blast and stays on until the Agency is satisfied that the children are not in harm's way. The rather obvious defences to Agency involvement in these situations involve *mea culpa* ("my fault") admissions and anger-management courses. If drugs or alcohol fuelled the incident, you will need to address these issues as well.

Radar sighting #7: School officials

As noted earlier, Agency workers often receive phone calls from school officials, perhaps to outline behavioural problems or perhaps to note truancy. Workers also visit a school when a teacher expresses concerns about a child. A regular assumption, and often a true one, holds that behavioural problems at school are likely a result of turmoil in the family. Sometimes the turmoil is serious, and teachers' observations often pinpoint children at risk. This assumption obviously penalizes families where the child's problems are medical, or say psychiatric, an assumption that may wrongly place blame on parenting skills. Nonetheless, radar sightings at the school do not normally result in an apprehension on their own, but these visits often generate Society visits to the parents and occasionally to neighbours.

Radar sighting #8: The next-door neighbour or the irate relative

A significant number of radar sightings result from concerned or irate neighbours or relatives who phone the Agency and express concern. Sometimes the calls are anonymous. The Agency must investigate. Family members provide the sort of insight into family problems that outsiders do not pick up on. Unfortunately, disputes between family members or arguments with neighbours can result in misleading or inappropriate allegations, but workers will assume the worst-case scenario because of potential risk to the child. The Agency must address all protection concerns in order to fulfill their mandate. Parents who react adversely to initial contacts by the Agency face the possibility of workers concluding that the children are indeed at risk and then having the Agency pursue the matter vigorously.

Radar sighting #9: The special-needs child

The special-needs child raises protection issues unlike any others, problems often extremely difficult to solve, problems foreshadowing tragedy on occasion. No other situation plants parents with normal or even outstanding parenting skills at risk to lose their child to the Agency. Two typical situations arise: service providers or professionals alert the Agency to the overwhelmed parent, or the overwhelmed parent on her own appeals to the Agency for assistance. Certainly, any special-needs child plunks extra pressure on parents. A single-parent family with other children in the home and a special-needs child bodes a recipe for disaster, often requiring superhuman duties from this parent. Such a parent perhaps possesses sufficient skills to parent a normal child or children, but the extra burden of the special-needs one increases the effort to a degree that raises protection concerns. This parent needs a supportive Agency worker, the support of professional service providers but also an extra-strong support group. This overburdened parent may simply throw in the towel and sign her child into care; the legislation in some jurisdictions specifically addresses this special circumstance and avoids the "protection" or "bad parent" stigma. This situation remains one of the few situations that can generate continuous, sometimes extraordinary help from the worker. But even when they sympathize with the struggling parent, the Agency must still address the protection issues to fulfill their mandate.

Radar sighting #10: Custody disputes

Custody disputes between parents result in many unfounded complaints to the Agency, complaints put forward by unscrupulous parents, complaints that waste an inordinate amount of Agency resources. In custody cases the status quo becomes an important consideration, so allegations against one parent of improper conduct that result in an Agency investigation may assist the other parent in their quest for custody. To elaborate, normally, the parent who has the child living with him or her possesses an advantage in a custody case, and some parents make allegations with a view to pushing forward their own case. By the time the Agency resolves a complaint, the status quo may be established, and subsequent custody proceedings become a formality. The worker may suspect a ruse, but the Agency still must address the allegations. Often an individual worker influences a custody case simply by threatening to apprehend the child, depending on who the child is placed with.

Five ways to alarm an agency worker

#1. Make your home a pigsty.

What does the Agency worker see when he or she visits the home? Often the worker's concern starts with something as basic as living arrangements. Occasionally he or she visits a home that is filthy and cluttered beyond belief. Is this your problem? In most cities, organizations exist to tackle this problem with little or no charge. Try the Salvation Army. The Salvation Army targets its services to the same basic group of people that the Agency does, but the Sally Ann possesses no gag reflex and no burning agenda contrary to a parent's interest. They will sometimes become involved in cleanup projects on a one-time basis. If not them, search out other help—but clean the home. Get some basic plan to keep it clean. It's prudent to keep Lysol® or pine-sol® cleaner on hand; the house should not only *be* clean, it should *smell* clean when the worker visits. Every lawyer acting for parents has viewed photos introduced by the Agency suggesting that hurricanes plunged into these particular houses. When such photos appear in court, you need to address the problem so that your lawyer can file the "after" photos. And waiting six months to file the "after" photos sends its own message to the court.

#2. Make the smell of your home knock the worker down.

Are you a first-generation immigrant? The home may have cooking or cultural input that affects the odour. Does the home smell non-Western to a young (read "inexperienced") worker? Take care to explain that these cooking odours or perfumes are common to your culture. The point is not to educate the worker in your culture but to help win the worker over to your side. Seek to make him or her an ally.

#3. Let children sleep on the floor.

Do you possess adequate beds and bedding for the kids? Community groups may help with this (and even furnish appropriate books and toys). Many places sell decent used furniture. Deal with these issues before they hit the Agency radar screen.

#4. Make sure your children smell.

Poverty smells. Money for soap and fancy detergent follows money for food in priority; every lawyer and worker employed in this area understands this fact. Lack of money does not fly as an excuse. Do not assume that your house doesn't smell or that your children don't. Every home smells of something, but staying off the radar could mean choosing the way your house and your children smell. When the worker starts poking around, invest in some disinfectant for the floors; it's an easy way to telegraph a message to the worker without speaking. This principle applies to other issues around the house as well. Do curtains grace your child's bedroom or just a sheet or flag tacked over the window? Few young Agency workers wouldn't draw some sort of adverse conclusion from stuff like this.

#5. Keep your children dirty.

Get those kids cleaned up and properly clothed. If you have a limited budget, get a church group to help with the clothes. If you plan to litigate with the Society, obtain your own support group. Canvas and consider the support programs that many church groups offer to a family, from babysitters to therapists to weekly outings. Praying or repenting may be optional. Many families turn things around in their fight against the Agency with the help of a supportive church group. There seldom are religious messages or any conditions attached to involvement with church groups; some groups just want to turn a good deed. And even if the group possesses a religious agenda, they are far less intrusive to deal with than the Agency. Getting your children looking presentable remains a chore, and finding appropriate clothing when they are growing like weeds is a constant battle, but presentable kids can help swing the worker over to your side. Short on money? Shop at the Sally Ann Thrift Stores (or any thrift shops), or haunt the St. Vincent de Paul societies or your local Goodwill.

How the Agency builds its case

A parlour game exists (often called "Operator") in which people gather in a circle and whisper a message from person to person. The end result is usually a garbled missive bearing no relationship to the original message. People repeat the message they thought they heard, and every person in the circle mangles the content of the message in some respect.

The same principle exists in a protection file. CAS workers, expert note takers from their university training, write down everything, and their filtered version of the conversation often bears no resemblance to the parent's filtered version—in fact, it rarely does. The material the Society files in court documents invariably results in an outburst from the parent: "I never said those things!" Defence lawyers encounter this reaction in virtually every case. It happens so often that it soon occurs to lawyers that this misperception can't always be the result of "evil" workers but may be due to stressful meetings and different agendas. Contrary to legislation and Agency propaganda, the workers' primary function is to gather evidence; they understand relevant facts and things that weave into the Agency's narrative; they intuitively fathom the best way to phrase their notes to advance the Agency's goals. When the client reviews these court documents, the misunderstanding often deepens the wedge between the worker and the client. Long before the Agency authorizes legal action, the notes going into the file build the case against the parents note by note.

When the Agency worker enters the home and finds the parent short of money for diapers or other things, he or she may offer friendly advice and perhaps some funds to solve the short-term problems. When the parent accepts the money, thinking, *What a great person*, the worker may note: "Cannot budget properly." In fact, the worker's notation rings true, but the only note resonating in the parent's mind is: "Worker helped today when I needed money for diapers."

The possibility of different interpretation exists in almost every entry into the file. The file against this parent is being built entry by entry. When the worker visits unannounced and observes that the house is a mess, he or she may note, "Poor housekeeping skills." When a mother yells at her child for dumping cereal on her sister's head, the worker may write, "Parenting skills suspect." If the mother ignores one of her children during the meeting, the notation could read, "Does not interact with youngest child; perhaps a poor bond." This is the way it goes. This is how the Agency builds cases—by Agency workers making notation after notation in your file.

It is guaranteed that most Agency workers with their university degrees make terrific note takers, the result of four to eight years of post-high school education. Add a few items from a criminal record, or a couple of police visits, and the result would throw Mother Teresa to the mat in a protection case. Workers may not scribble the notes at the time of the incident, but they are usually recorded while the incidents are fresh in the worker's mind—although already out of the parent's. Six months or a year later, your memory may be foggy on the incident, but those notes drop into court if the Agency starts litigation. Workers may not accumulate this file information with any nefarious plan in mind; they simply understand their job: collect information to assist in the future. They fully appreciate that any such notes come into relevance in any protection application; this is a major part of their job. The case against you is always simmering along, being built by the worker, sentence by sentence, clause by clause, word by word, and bubbling along until the Agency pops it into court.

The parent who plays defence

Some parents decide from the onset to play defence and avoid confrontation and court battles with the Society. The parent who chooses to play defence, with or without counsel, often thinks as follows:

1. I hate the Agency, but I cooperate with the Agency, sign the releases requested and agree to whatever testing is appropriate, given the facts.
2. I hate the worker, but I make friends with him or her. While I may not be invited to his or her wedding, I will convince the worker of my parenting skills; I will convey that I am capable of appropriate responses to standard parenting situations.
3. I do not ask for a new worker under any circumstance— repeat, under *any circumstance*. Please reread this. As a lawyer in this area, I am unaware of any exception to this rule. The Agency routinely refuses these requests, which the worker learns of, and serves only to alien- ate her; *you understand—it alienates her big-time*. To restate this rule once more: workers are not replaced as the result of parents' complaints. In fact, in my experience workers are responsible for the return of far more kids than the most eloquent and diligent lawyer, so chum up to her.

4. I *definitely* do not complain about the worker—to his or her supervisor or anyone else in the Agency.
5. I don't do anything that will result in a bad note. I address and reconsider any contentious conduct at once.
6. I sign up for every course the Agency recommends.
7. I attend every session of all courses and participate vigorously.

And here is the most important, but perhaps the most difficult, rule of all:

8. I am entirely happy about the courses, the Agency and the worker. When asked, I do not think, *I don't want to suck up to them.* I think, *I love my children enough to walk on hot coals for them, and I surely can suffer the attentions of a pushy protection worker.* "May I offer you some cookies and tea?"

Please review the Orlando option in a previous chapter if you wish to revisit the philosophy behind these rules.

Chapter 3

The Apprehension and Temporary (or Interim) Care

The apprehension

Most court cases commence with an apprehension. Typically this occurs when the worker appears before a justice of the peace or a judge, files an affidavit (a statement of sworn facts) outlining his or her concerns and obtains a warrant to apprehend the child. In many cases, a police officer initiates the procedure with a call to the Agency. But in most situations, the worker comes to the home with a police officer and picks up the child. The child is dropped into foster care, and the matter arrives in court within a few days. The parent likely knew nothing of this court attendance to obtain this warrant; no one spoke up for him or her at this stage, so no one pressed his side of the story before the justice granted the warrant. Railing against this step in the process serves no useful purpose. The parent should hunt up a lawyer. The court case concerning his child has begun.

The first court date

Many parents attend the first court date assuming that they will be allowed to argue the merits of their file at that time, that justice will prevail, their children will be returned and the Agency will be handed its head on a platter. In fact, the only material before the justice at the first court appearance will be the countless pages filed by the Agency. In front of the judge rests a stack of other matters he or she needs to deal with that day. In most cases, the only thing parents obtain at the first court date is a future court date to argue about the temporary care of their children. The date must be far enough away to allow time to hunt up a lawyer and file papers outlining their side of the story. The system strikes most parents as unfair, but so is life. The children will remain in care until the parents enter into an agreement with the Agency or until they file material with the court and argue for temporary care in front of a judge. At the interim hearing, the judge will review written material and often does not hear witnesses. Unless the case is overwhelming, the children will be ordered into care pending agreement between the parties or a trial.

Time limits

Time limits in child-protection cases are determined by the legislation in each jurisdiction and by the rules of the court. Courts routinely want to push these cases along more quickly than other cases, because children in care remain under obvious stress. Whether the children return to their parents or temporarily remain in care, judges do seek to resolve the issue as soon as possible. But all court cases flow through imperfect court systems, systems that routinely deal with large numbers of files and the conflicting time schedules of lawyers and judges. Court papers served on you indicate time limits—read them carefully. Time limits in protection matters generally start to run from the date of service, but you should address the timelines in your case at your first meeting with your lawyer.

Where to stick agency material

The initial paperwork served on a parent contains mountains of pages. It is not unknown for it to exceed 50 or 60 pages, or to push 100 if the parents have developed an ongoing relationship with the Agency. Copy the material and save the original for your lawyer. Write the date of service on the first page, and start to provide comprehensive written responses to the Agency material, for your lawyer. The material served usually falls into one of two categories: "pleadings," the material that outlines the Agency's position in the court case, and temporary "motion material," the material that will help determine where the child resides until the parties come to agreement or a judge hears evidence at the trial and decides.

Discussing court material and issues with children

Here is an issue that parents sometimes fail to grasp: material served by the Agency, or the issues raised in the parents' court battle with the Agency, remains "adult content only" and not subject matter for discussions with children under the age of majority. While involving your adult children in these discussions remains perfectly acceptable, discussions with younger children telegraphs a clear message about your parenting skills, namely that they lack maturity. No exceptions to this rule appear to exist, even if one of the children is your best friend. If the proceedings involve children old enough for their own lawyer, the court appoints counsel to represent them—but the rule still applies.

Pleadings

Court pleadings carry a simple function: to outline the positions of the parties. The Agency's pleadings outline the Agency's case against you, and your pleadings respond to their pleadings and set out your position. Pleadings deal with facts—often perceived facts. Agency pleadings set out the facts they rely on and the remedy they seek. Your pleadings set out the facts you rely on and the remedy you seek, which is normally to have the children returned or some less intrusive order brought than the one sought by the Agency. In protection cases, you need to do more than simply deny the allegations against you; you must answer the allegations and outline the facts and your position clearly. If the Agency alleges a drug addiction, their pleadings set out the facts that give rise to their concerns. Your response, set out in sufficient detail, may deny the problem, put forth the facts that you rely on and challenge their facts. Perhaps you agree to periodic testing. Or perhaps your pleadings admit to a drug problem and indicate a treatment program that addresses the addiction.

The court expects to read the pleadings of all sides and understand the issues that separate the parties in your particular court case. The pleadings possess different names, depending upon your jurisdiction, and these names occasionally change to reflect popular philosophies, but in adversarial systems, their function remains the same: to set out the position of the parties based upon the facts outlined. The document originating a court case may be called a Statement of Claim, or an Application, or something else, depending on where you hail from, and your response may be called an Answer, Answer and Plan of Care, Statement of Defence or Response. But whatever the name, the document you provide serves the same basic purpose. It helps identify and outline the issues between you and the Agency. Fundamental to your pleadings is a simple recitation of the facts you rely on. The arguments made by the parties or counsel down the road will rely largely on the facts pleaded, and to a great degree they will be circumscribed by them.

Interim or Temporary Care Hearing

Ideally, at the first court date all parties appear properly prepared—neckties in place, demure skirts flicking, all pleadings served and filed, all lawyers primed and ready to argue about . . . well, I guess, maybe . . . argue about these kids. *Doesn't happen!*

At the first court date, the Agency's court paperwork may yet have to be served upon you; it remains unfiled with the court and therefore unread by the judge. You may have fought through the legal-aid system but still be seeking a lawyer, who will require time to review the Agency material and craft a response with you. Expect two or three adjournments and an elapsed time of three to four weeks or more before anything of substance is argued. During this period, a temporary order will likely keep the children with strangers in foster care while your access to them is limited to brief periods of time only and perhaps supervised. It is not fair, but that's the way it is.

After the apprehension, usually at the first court hearing, the judge will set a date to hear argument on the Temporary Care Hearing (also called the Temporary-Care Motion, Presentation Hearing, the Interim Care or Temporary Guardianship Hearing, depending on the jurisdiction). Courts try to schedule the Temporary-Care Motion as soon as possible, but this date may be a few weeks or perhaps a month or two away, depending on the facts and the schedule of the court and the lawyers.

The day of the Temporary-Care hearing is usually the first time that you have a realistic chance of arguing for the return of your child. This hearing decides who will have care of the child until the trial or some other resolution of the matter. Will the child stay in care of the Agency, be returned to the parent, or be placed somewhere else? Other issues come into play at this hearing as well. Will the court appoint a lawyer for any older children? Are police records or those of doctors or other experts to be examined? The judge typically tries to deal not only with the temporary placement of and access to the child but with as many other things as possible to push the case along. Generally, argument proceeds on the affidavit evidence filed by the parties, often without oral evidence, although the judge controls the process and possesses wide latitude in what he or she considers in arriving at a decision.

Trials can be anywhere from six months to a year or more away, so the issue of temporary care becomes very important. If the child is returned to you, it sends a clear message to the Agency that they should try to resolve the matter short of trial, as the judge has no immediate protection concerns. This shows that the Agency's case is a little weak. If the child is placed in the temporary care of the Agency, it telegraphs *your* need to address some serious issues on a timely basis. But the issue during argument of the Temporary-Care Motion remains the same as always—namely, can you and your lawyer give a comfort level to the motions judge about the risk to the child, pending a final resolution? The chances of this happening without the parent taking the stand are slim. If the allegations are serious—allegations of abuse resulting in substantial harm to the child, for instance—then I suggest the answer is really nil rather than slim.

Clearly, a child placed in the temporary care of the Agency advances the Agency's case more often than the parents'. As well, it sends the message that, after reviewing all parties' positions, the court retains concerns about risk to the child. Some cases collapse at this point. But consider the situation of a child inflicted with behavioural problems whose parents' skills appear marginal. Unless professional help addresses the child's issues on a timely basis, the child's problems will worsen while he or she is in care, making it even harder for those parents to demonstrate the necessary skills to manage the child. While the Agency's temporary care of a child *in theory* allows those problems to be addressed quickly, so that logically the parents can gain traction in their quest to deal with the child properly, a timely approach is highly unlikely. In all likelihood, the child's behaviour will worsen in temporary care, harming the parents' case. And, sad to say, once the parties lock in serious court combat, they usually focus on the battle rather than on the child, and each side hardens its position on the issues.

The alternate caregiver

If the Agency's material contains serious allegations that might resonate with the court and seem difficult to address before argument of the interim motion, there may be a way to sidestep the draconian remedy of your child being taken into the Agency's care. This involves a proposal to the Agency or to the court that the children be placed in the care of relatives or friends. Of course, this placement requires court approval once litigation has begun. Acknowledging the likelihood of Agency success at the Motion for Interim (or Temporary) Care often allows consideration of possible alternative placements. Before argument of the Temporary-Care Motion, you have something to negotiate with, since the Agency cannot be absolutely certain of success. This slight edge disappears if the court finds in favour of the Agency's views and orders your child into care. Perhaps as part of the Temporary-Care Motion you should present other caregivers as an alternative placement should the court doubt your version of events. Do you or your partner possess a sparkling sibling with children the same age? Perhaps that sibling (or grandparent, in-law, etc.) should put forth a plan to have the child placed with him or her on a temporary basis. The Agency may agree, but even if they don't, the judge might. Very often the Agency's position sends a message about their long-term flexibility in your case. If they resist a reasonable placement of the child with a friend or family member who looks good by all objective standards, does it indicate that they intend to take this case all the way to trial?

The person put forth as temporary caregiver needs to file an affidavit with the court that includes a Plan of Care and background material. This material must be filed early enough to allow the Agency time to investigate the person and home prior to the Interim-Care Motion; otherwise, the matter will drive yet another adjournment. Preparation of plans of care is dealt with below. As part of the material filed in support of an alternative placement, there should be fairly standard undertakings by the person filing the plan. The alternate caregiver must indicate a willingness to follow a court order, say with respect to access, even if the terms of the court order are not to his or her liking. Courts consider placements that minimize disruption to the child, so the caregiver will need to address this issue. Will the children stay in the same school, be with the same friends and so on? When proposed alternate caregivers are seen to be reputable and upstanding, without criminal record or Agency background, and the plan of care is comprehensive, the children will often be placed with them, sometimes with the consent of the Agency but surprisingly often without.

Motions

A *motion* is simply a request, usually a temporary (or interim) one, to a judge, which does not normally resolve the matter but pushes the case along in some way. In the Temporary-Care situation, you might request that the child stay with you or an alternate caregiver, while the Agency requests that the child remain in their care. As noted, the motion documents may address more than just temporary care of the child. Typical requests include access to the child, perhaps a call for drug testing of a parent, or the appointment of a lawyer for the child. These are all temporary matters that ultimately push the court file toward resolution or trial.

Affidavits

Legal talk: "Affidavit." Expanding on the previous definition, an affidavit is a statement of facts someone has sworn to be true. The statement is "sworn" (i.e., you must "swear" or "affirm," in front of a person authorized to swear or commission affidavits in your jurisdiction, that the document is true). There are serious consequences—penal provisions in all jurisdictions—for swearing a false affidavit.

When you bring a motion asking for something from the court, you must file a sworn affidavit supporting that request. You may file more than one affidavit in support of a motion. People at the local courthouse can normally assist in swearing affidavits for self-represented people. Attach relevant documents to your affidavit; such documents become *exhibits* to be sworn as well.

When to gloat after a Temporary-Care Motion

Depending on the facts, you can sometimes prevail at a Temporary-Care hearing. You may have well-documented material or a great plan of care; perhaps you have a competent alternative caregiver or an articulate argument by you or your counsel. This does not conclude the matter. If you do prevail at the Temporary-Care Motion, rather than gloating, you should approach the worker or their lawyer and offer something more to them—such as a slightly more intrusive role in your life—even though you "won" the motion. Here is the reason. Any appeal would be to a higher court. The feeling among many lawyers is that appeal courts do not have the same feel for the dynamics of child-protection cases that courts of first instance do, and so are reluctant to interfere with the lower court's decision. Most lawyers would prefer to resolve the matter in the lower courts. So if you possess the upper hand, perhaps you should use it wisely and consider it a bargaining chip.

The Hearing for Temporary Care

At the Temporary-Care hearing, lawyers and parents attend court. The motions and affidavits, every piece of paper, are all neat and pretty, with perfect punctuation; all are served and filed and before the court. Everyone passes into the courtroom, finely dressed and buttoned-down for argument. The weakness of the system bites you in the butt once the motion argument begins. You, the parent, do not speak if you have a lawyer. Whether or not you have a lawyer, in most cases you do not take the witness stand to tell your story. In the land of the Charter of Rights and Freedoms, you do not, as yet, have the right to take the witness stand at a Temporary-Care hearing. It's a grim fact that in a Temporary-Care proceeding, often no one takes the witness stand and no one gives oral evidence; the lawyers argue about the pieces of paper that have been filed. Your child's life is decided by those pieces of paper, most of which you disagree with. Here is a thought for the people who draft these protection laws or for any lawyer considering a Charter case: *A parent should have an absolute right to take the witness stand and give oral evidence at a Temporary-Care hearing.*

This system works in the Agency's favour more than yours. Nobody in court suggests that the Agency will hurt your child if they win the motion, but the Agency suggests that you may harm your child if you win. In most cases with serious allegations, judges are loath to return children without getting the full measure of a parent in, say, three or four hours of testimony at trial. Disputes involving credibility on a motion are, in practice, resolved in the Agency's favour.

The system works somewhat better when the issues involve objective third-party evidence: doctors' reports, affidavits from a teacher, or letters from community-service providers; in short, any collateral reports or letters by third-party experts or near-experts that address the protection issues. Procedure on these Temporary-Care proceedings varies from jurisdiction to jurisdiction and court to court; some courts accept letters filed on behalf of the parents, and some require that the information be reduced to affidavit form. Most courts expect lawyers to file material in affidavit form, but they might bend the rules a bit and accept letters filed by self-represented parents. Courts occasionally adjourn Temporary-Care Motions to allow additional evidence, but this remains completely discretionary. A collateral issue at these hearings is access to the child. You should assess the issue of access at the time of drafting the material for the Temporary-Care Motion, keeping in mind the possibility that the Agency might prevail.

Mothers who are breastfeeding or wish to breastfeed need to raise this in their initial material, as a court might alter the access provisions to accommodate you. Access to a young child needs to be frequent, commencing at the earliest possibility, and this issue should be raised with the worker even before the first court date.

Chapter 4

Access

The strategy of access

In the great majority of child-protection cases, no final resolution occurs during the early stages of the court battle. The Agency files pieces of paper, the parent files pieces of paper, lawyer-type yapping goes on and the judge reviewing all those conflicting messages possesses a fragile awareness of the merits of each side. Judges normally yearn to hear the evidence of each side, view the witnesses eyeball to eyeball, judge credibility and review all of the evidence before making decisions affecting the child. This is the nature of the process; it's a lengthy, awkward process, with no feasible alternative system in the works.

To repeat: in a seriously contested protection matter, where contradictory evidence spills out in front of a judge and there is no alternate caregiver that the court finds appropriate, the child most often goes into the temporary care of the Agency. Accordingly, the issue of access takes on critical importance at this stage, and the motion for temporary care and the hearing often revolve as much around this issue as around the temporary care. The decision of this hearing in terms of access usually pushes one party's case or the other party's case from this point forward.

Hello! Provincial and territorial governments fund agencies, and governments never possess unlimited funds. When the Agency manages the access visits, it costs the Agency money and some of the concern about access may be a function of this reality. If you seek unreasonable access, you may be rejected just because of the burden it places upon the Agency, a burden of both finances and personnel. But in truth, most courts place little weight on the cost of access.

Specified access

Most temporary orders specify access in absolute terms: "The mother shall have access for a minimum of three days per week, for a minimum of two hours per visit," or "The father shall have eight hours unsupervised access to the child, every other weekend, at the father's place of residence." If the access concerns an older child, the access may be, "Subject to the wishes of the child." Access to a special-needs child who is apprehended because of parental burnout may contain no restrictions at all. Where one parent displays problems—perhaps an abusive nature, perhaps an anger problem, perhaps drug or alcohol addiction—the parents often receive different access arrangements.

Access at the discretion of the Agency

This remains a recipe for subsequent litigation, but it is something many parents agree with in the hope of mollifying the Agency and perhaps gaining concessions down the road. In practice, this approach rarely bears fruit; parents should seek specified access. In fact, it is rare for the Agency's view of appropriate access to accord with that of a parent once the parties engage in litigation. Most lawyers recommend and seek specified access for their clients and refuse to accept anything less, preferring to argue the matter in court.

Supervised access

Supervised access comes in a variety of forms. In some cases, the Agency seeks access supervised at their facility and supervised by their employees. In such cases, assume that the Agency observes and makes notes at each access visit and may introduce these observations in subsequent court appearances. The Agency observations may include such utterings as, "The mother failed to hug the child," or "The child refused to interact with the father" or "The father said the following inappropriate things . . ." At some point, maybe even at trial, the court might consider such evidence, so appropriate conduct at supervised-access visits becomes important.

Changing the access at some future time normally involves a material change in the facts, which is a burden not too difficult to meet where most judges are concerned—for instance, the parent has consistently tested negative for drugs or alcohol or has completed an anger-management course or engaged in other remedial action. But a valid reason or change should precede the request; usually that some aspect of risk has been adequately addressed by the parent.

What not to do at supervised-access visits

Sustaining the parent-child bond remains the primary purpose of access visits and the secondary one is to comfort the child. Parents using the visit to advance their case often wind up achieving the opposite. It is inappropriate to tape, videotape, record or photograph such visits, regardless of what you hope to achieve through such conduct. If you desire to photograph your child, seek permission first. The proper agenda during access visits is to demonstrate appropriate bonds with your child and to convey appropriate parenting responses to any given situation that arises. The period that a child is in care could extend from several weeks to six months to two years, and this extended time frame poses difficulty for parents. Some days the access drags, and some days it scoots by; demonstrating appropriate conduct on every occasion poses a continuous long-term challenge, a fact experienced judges will take note of, to some degree. Access visits, above all else, give you an opportunity to demonstrate commitment to your child. And bear in mind that notes taken during access visits become available to either party for admission at trial.

Too much access

The concept of *too much* access arises in a few ways. Access to a child outside your normal home situation is artificial. Sitting in a room at the Agency with an observer taking notes about everything you say and do makes 60 minutes stretch into a lifetime. Parenting skills remain an issue in a protection application, and interactions between you and your child count as fair game. But undertake a realistic review of your schedule before entering into any agreement regarding access. Can you physically attend all the access visits for which you are negotiating? Missed visits generate notes to the file and may ultimately form part of the Agency's case. The rather obvious issue is this: what sort of a parent misses access visits to a child in care? A better approach would be to take somewhat fewer access visits, show no missed visits, and display great attitude at each and every visit. I guarantee you the fact you missed access visits will pop up at trial—in addition to any other problems encountered during visits.

When the Agency holds deep concerns about basic parenting skills, its workers may offer large amounts of access, to see if their concerns are justified. If you accept such an offer, consider whether you need to address certain issues or seek backup help before you agree to it. They may offer large amounts of access time to set you up for failure. A failure to maintain access visits may fatally taint your chances at trial. Of course, showing up at access visits with liquor on your breath or spaced out on drugs does your case no good; likewise, displays of anger return to haunt you at trial. If your plan of care proposed another person, say a grandparent or close friend, to assist you in the care of your child, try to gain access for that person. People not specified in the order bear no right to visit a child in care.

Additional access issues

Access visits form a key part of the strategy in a protection case. Access visits telegraph a relationship with your child as few other facts can. Access visits help you or hurt you, but they are always an important consideration. As noted, the Agency makes notes on every supervised access visit, potentially with a view to their admission into evidence. Irregular access visits or a pattern of being consistently late to visits warrants a notation in the file. Appropriate interaction between you and your child advances your case. Hugging is allowed and expected, but yelling at or berating your child is a serious negative. The Agency tolerates criticism of, say, the prime minister, but criticism of the Agency itself or the worker will be noted and may ultimately return to hurt you in the following way: a judge considering the return of a child to you, subject to supervision by the Agency, may have serious concerns about how well you could work with the Agency. With all the baggage set out above, access becomes exceedingly trying, but as a devoted parent, you will treat it as an opportunity.

After you file your material for the Temporary-Care Motion, it's time to engage in a brutal reality check, preferably with your counsel. Pray that your lawyer rises to the challenge and slaps some hard truths at you. An experienced, clued-in lawyer knows the odds and can sense whether or not the Agency will prevail with the Temporary-Care Motion—to wit whether the court will order the child into care, return the child to you, or perhaps place the child with a proposed alternate caregiver. In most cases the Agency succeeds at the Temporary-Care Motion and the child drops into the foster-care system. If your lawyer thinks this likely in your case, you should negotiate access before the motion. Even though the Agency possesses a good case for temporary care, they can't be absolutely sure they will prevail. In return for your consent, they are likely to bend somewhat on the access and provide you with access that works for you and pushes your agenda. Should you fail to take advantage of this opportunity to horse-trade, you could face a more difficult time by the time the trial rolls around. This issue alone shows the advantage in seeking out experienced legal counsel in protection matters. Infrequent visitors to child-protection cases seldom appreciate the nuances of temporary access until it is too late. By way of observation, competent lawyers will file material in preparation for a Temporary-Care Motion before negotiating the issues in play. Among other reasons, they do this to increase their client's leverage during these negotiations.

General rules for access

1. A parent is better served if the access is specified and set out in a court order.
2. A child is better served with frequent access to the parents—as frequent as possible—even if supervised at the Agency.
3. A clued-in parent refrains from discussing the court case during access visits.
4. A clued-in parent refrains from complaining about the Agency or workers during access visits.
5. A clued-in parent understands that access visits directly affect subsequent court proceedings.
6. A clued-in parent constructively uses the time the child is in care. Having limited time with the child frees up time to take that parenting course, or to kick that habit or to participate in that anger-management course.

Chapter 5

Plans of Care

In my experience, judges actually read plans of care. When the Agency institutes protection proceedings against you and you seek the return of your child, you should file a plan of care with the court, both for the motion for temporary care and in the pleadings that outline your case. A plan of care outlines how you intend to care for your child and addresses the issues in play. A plan of care normally is a statement of facts, with a few good intentions tossed in.

A court typically remains sceptical about a plan that relies on too many good intentions. The Agency or the parent generally files a plan of care, but any person seeking to have a child placed with him or her can file a plan with the Agency and often with the court. The plan of care demonstrates the capabilities of the proposed caregiver in light of the needs of this particular child. If more than one child is involved, each child's needs can be addressed separately, and the plan of care presents an opportunity to demonstrate the relationship between the proposed caregiver and each child. Ideally, it also demonstrates a grasp of the issues involved, including any of the parenting or child-behaviour issues raised in the Agency's material.

Every plan contains certain basic matters to be addressed, and I set out the rudiments below, but anything relevant to the care of your child is germane. A plan of care filed with the court must sometimes be in affidavit form, but sometimes a court form exists. In every case, you must take care to accurately and adequately describe your plan to care for this child. A person who is already party to the protection application can file a plan of care, but a person seeking to be added as a party should also include in the court submission a carefully drafted plan as part of his or her material. Plans of care often suggest more than one caregiver or assisting caregiver, and in cases where the Agency raises serious parenting concerns, this is almost mandatory.

Best interest of the child

The underlying precept in a plan of care revolves around one basic issue, so scream it out: "My plan, Your Honour—hear me loud and clear, damn-it-all—is in the best interests of this child!" So set out—proclaim!—in clear and unambiguous terms that your plan is in the best interests of the child, and reinforce that in the material that follows. Be aware that any sort of expressed or implied suggestion that the real purpose of the plan is to address your own needs is counterproductive and will raise concerns about your grasp of the issues involved in this protection case.

Who are the proposed caregivers?

A proper plan of care begins with identifying the proposed caregivers and their relationship to the children. "I am the paternal grandmother of . . . ," or "I was the next-door neighbour, and the children resided with me for xx months after xx." Make it crystal clear to the court what your blood or adoptive or historic relationship or connection is to the child or children. Fess up to any criminal record problem in the past, or, indeed, to any serious blemishes at all. You can explain an offence several years in the past involving drinking and driving, but criminal offences involving children preclude a proposed caregiver from making a credible pitch for the child. In such a case, revise the plan of care for the child and perhaps propose alternate caregivers. A rule of thumb: insisting that you were not guilty, even though you were found guilty of or pleaded guilty to a criminal offence, wastes everyone's time in any child-protection matter.

The ties that bind

The plan must also address the historic love and emotional ties of the proposed caregiver to the children. Outline how long you and the have children lived together, and outline the nature of your emotional connection to the children. Outline as well the nature of the bond between the children and caregiver. Courts recognize the bonds that exist between the children and other siblings or half-siblings who reside in the home; outline in detail the stabilizing nature of those bonds. Perhaps older siblings will live with the children in your proposed plan, and perhaps those siblings will harbour a nurturing relationship with the children. While you may think it's obvious, outline the exact nature of the relationship between the proposed caregiver and the children. An expression of love for the children and a detailed outline of the emotional connections between everyone who sharing the residence are matters for the plan, including stepparents or live-in spouses and offspring.

A child apprehended from the custodial parent poses extra problems for the non-custodial parent seeking to have the child placed with him or her, so discuss the relationship developed during access visits and holidays. If there has been no access—say when the non-custodial parent has not been in the child's life—discuss a method to restart this relationship: for instance, demonstrate a knowledge of the child's current needs and care, given his or her age.

The wishes of the child

Older children can have input about their living arrangements. A child of twelve with no emotional problems or mental disabilities will have his or her wishes considered by the court, and other children close to that age may also be entitled to their opinions. If your child is of this age or close to it and clearly expresses a desire to live with you or the proposed caregiver, set this information out in the plan.

Stability

Perhaps the most consistent issue with regard to the placement of a child is stability. Courts routinely put a premium on providing the most stable life possible for a child. If your child has lived in a stable home environment with one of the proposed caregivers, describe this in detail for the court. Include details that address the continuing presence of the same people, as well as schools, churches, or activities in the child's life—anything that conveys the message that the child lives in a stable situation and that this stable condition will continue if the court places the child with you or the proposed caregiver.

Guidance through life

A good plan to care for children includes a comprehensive outline for the child's future. Outline the educational plans for your child; this is an especially serious matter for special-needs children. For example, what sports does your child enjoy, and how will you maintain this connection? Set out any special interests of your child and how you will accommodate them in the future. Consider the moral issues that should be addressed, such as attendance and participation at churches, mosques, or synagogues. Does the child have a special cultural background that can be addressed? A parent proposing a plan of care has a unique opportunity to craft a plan that addresses that child's problems as well as special interests and distinctive gifts, in light of the abilities of the person proposing the plan. In the development of this plan, if you have been involved in your child's life, you are in a perfect position to craft a statement that reflects and screams a message about your relationship.

The necessities of life

The plan should address the basic economic issues that face all families: how to feed, clothe, and shelter them, in the present and for the years to come. A mansion and chauffeured rides to school are not necessary for your plan, but do indicate the source of your money. Do you have a stable financial plan to provide for the child? Are you in a position to provide some sort of college fund? Are you on welfare? Are you on a disability pension? Being on public assistance will not necessarily sink a plan, unless it somehow relates to protection issues. For a child of tender years, you should perhaps indicate that you own a proper crib, bassinet, bedding and clothes.

Males and infants of tender years

If a male parent seeks placement of a baby, he should pay special attention to setting out where he has acquired his caregiving skills. Judges accept a male in a primary caregiving role for a child of tender years, but it would be unwise to assume that hidden biases don't occasionally twist the issues. As in all plans, you should set out how your life skills apply to comprehensively address the child's needs.

The home

A good plan of care describes the child's home; having the largest home on the block is rarely a deciding factor. How many bedrooms does the home have? Are smoke alarms and carbon monoxide detectors in place? Do you own the home? If the home is an apartment, point out any advantages of the apartment, such as controlled access or on-site facilities such as game rooms or laundry rooms. Situations in which the proposed caregiver is seeking a new home or apartment pose more of a problem. Simply set out the sort of accommodations that you seek. If an Agency worker has inspected the home, indicate so. And identify each and every person who will reside in the home with the child.

Clothing, toys and accessories

Every child needs certain basic material goods to survive and to succeed in life. Do you have, or can you obtain, proper clothing or bedding for the child? Do you have age-appropriate toys? Is there a computer at the home? Setting out the items that a child needs to flourish demonstrates to the court that you understand the child's current and future needs. A child deeply involved in soccer, for example, has different material needs than an avid chess fanatic or one living for the latest fashion craze.

Dental and medical care

A good plan of care addresses the caregiver's preparedness with respect to medical and dental issues of the child. Will your medical plan cover the child? If the child possesses an existing dentist or doctor, indicate so. If not, set out the steps to find this care. Does the child have a relationship with any experts who are currently addressing the child's mental or physical health issues? Demonstrate a comprehensive knowledge about these issues. How close are clinics and hospitals to your home, in case of emergency?

Special-needs children

A special-needs child often requires special apparatus or therapy and maybe unique programs or extra assistance. Are these items available in/to your home? Have you identified the programs that the child needs and lined up assistance? For a special-needs child, it is also important to have thought about future needs and future options as well. A parent holds special insight into his or her child's needs and should demonstrate this insight in the plan of care.

Health and education of proposed caregivers

A good plan of care refers to the health and education of the proposed caregivers. Confirm that you have no health problems impacting on child care abilities, or include details about how you will address or minimize the effect of any problems. A lack of education will not disqualify you as a caregiver, but it may require addressing the issue specifically. While the court would not preclude a person unable to read or write from having a child placed with him or her, it would be prudent to have assisting caregivers as backup. A caregiver with a disability should also address his or her disability in the plan of care.

Special skills of proposed caregivers

If you possess parenting diplomas and they are available, attach copies of them to the plan. Certain professions suggest training that implicitly affects child care above and beyond the training most parents have. Professional fields, such as medicine or nursing and perhaps physiotherapy, the ministry and a few others fall into this category and should be mentioned specifically. Having raised other children successfully carries a certain weight, so mention this along with details of the children raised. For example, "I raised two other children: my son xxx, who is employed as xxx, and my daughter xxx, who is currently enrolled in university."

Schools

A plan of care that provides for the child to continue in his or her existing school with current friends and teachers pulls in bonus points for stability. A plan calling for the child to attend a different school suggests that the proposed caregiver has contacted the new school, scoped out the programs and transfer requirements and perhaps met and discussed the child with the new teacher. Detail these efforts in the plan.

Activities of the child

Children require a certain amount of organized activity, and the plan of care should address these matters, with the child's inclinations and local opportunities in mind. The following list should serve as a checklist only: going to the park, games, reading, bowling, athletic activities, walking, library visits, watching educational programs on TV or DVDs, playing musical instruments, church activities, swimming, beach, school activities and visiting grandparents and other family.

Relationship to agency

Many protection cases involve ongoing Agency input after a court order is made. Judges need to know whether you can work with the Agency after the court makes an order. At a minimum, You should indicate a willingness to sign whatever releases or directions the Agency requests, whether for teachers, doctors or any other professionals involved with the child. Consent in your plan to Agency visits to the home, both announced and unannounced. The plan also provides an opportunity to set out mea culpas (admissions of fault): "I enrolled in a program that addresses alcohol abuse," or "I attend an anger-management course."

Culturally significant plans of care

Cultural considerations in plans of care can influence court decisions. This applies to plans concerning not only a First Nations, Inuit or Métis child but also any child in whose life the cultural aspect reigns as an important feature. Will the child be nurtured in this way in the future by the person proposing the plan? If no past cultural exposure exists (for instance, if the custodial parent did not embrace these values), the issue may not be as important but may still bear relevance. Stability involves helping the child know where he or she fits in the world, and cultural values can play into that issue. So any plan with cultural aspects should be phrased accordingly, setting out the unique values that will assist that child in life. The plan should demonstrate above all else that the benefits of the culture are positive and, beyond that, that they will be beneficial to this particular child now and in the years to come. Such a plan might include the family backgrounds and traditions and outline who is the "keeper" of this culture in the community. Is it the reserve, the local community centre, the church, the mosque, the synagogue, the shaman or perhaps extended family or an association? The plan should deal with extended family in detail, as these people normally reinforce those values. How will the proposed caregivers reinforce the culture in the context of the protection issues that a court will be considering? While the court will note cultural aspects, these aspects should only form a small part of a well-crafted plan of care and not overpower other aspects of the plan.

Undertakings

The comprehensive plan of care should include undertakings, or promises, to address certain issues if the child is placed with you. The following undertakings for caregivers outline the more common relevant issues to be set out clearly for the court: Undertake to keep the home clean in accordance with acceptable community standards; undertake to conduct food shopping on a regular basis, with the child's nutritional needs as the first priority; undertake to keep the child in clean clothes, to bathe a young child regularly and to seek out appropriate medical checkups and appointments with the family doctor; undertake to arrange for a family dentist and regular checkups.

For the child of tender years, the caregiver should acknowledge an understanding of an infant's needs. An infant needs foods delivered on a regular basis; needs a schedule; needs regular feedings of good, proper food; needs diapers and outfits changed regularly and needs proper amounts of sleep.

Bottom line: plans of care

A court rarely returns a child as a result of a plan of care regardless of how eloquent, but a plan of care presents a perfect venue to convey to the court that you possess the full measure of knowledge about your child and a grasp of the issues involved. A plan of care that addresses protection issues in a comprehensive fashion sets the stage for a parent to address those issues at trial—the goal, of course, being to provide a comfort level to the trial judge.

Chapter 6

The Parenting Capacity Assessment

The legal system abounds in experts—*pooh-bahs*, if you will. But do not lose sight of this fact: the ultimate expert in a protection case remains the judge hearing the case. In protection cases, the *other* expert most often relied upon remains the clinical psychologist, who is called to identify risk in a protection proceeding, to render a judgment on the needs of a child, to flash expertise on the ability of a parent to meet those needs and to highlight the gap between those issues.

Like everyone else in the system, the clinical psychologist usually errs on the side of caution. But the decision to do such an assessment exposes another sad, perhaps ugly but unavoidable side of the system. Would it offend anyone if I pointed out that many lawyers in the protection field do not feast at the top end of the legal pecking order? Most lawyers hacking away on protection files receive payment from the provincial or territorial legal-aid system; few of these lawyers made the law review; few wrote those pithy articles that light up the eyes and brains of the Supreme Court—but they all need to make a living. Some lawyers like the work and flail away incessantly to help their clients (I personally know of two . . . maybe three), but some don't. Some, apparently, convince their clients to consent to an assessment while knowing they will fare miserably. And those lawyers, so it is said, will use the results of an assessment to beat their client up into consenting to what the Agency wants. Failing that, these lawyers may provoke a disagreement that results in the lawyer being able to get off the record, and this is the point at which many people become unrepresented by counsel. This is the way the system works. Suck it up and soldier on. Your child is at stake.

Any parent being counselled by his or her lawyer to consent to such an assessment should reflect on the above before actually consenting. (The consequences of a failure to consent to a court-ordered assessment are set out below.) The Society succeeds, in many cases, because a parent fares poorly in a Parenting Capacity Assessment. An assessment is not sought in every case, but when there are allegations of serious risk to the child, and where they involve parenting issues, the Agency often requests an assessment. May we be so bold as to suggest that they usually request an assessment when they think it will push their case?

An assessor routinely requires full disclosure from all of the parties before agreeing to conduct an assessment, so everything—absolutely everything—is on the table. Plans of Care put forward by the parent or other proposed caregiver are pinned under the assessor's microscope. The assessor reviews any community or personal support available to a person proposing a plan. You can expect that the assessor enjoys complete access to all of the court papers filed and to the entire child-protection file as well, including all allegations made to the Agency over the years, even anonymously. And, of course, you have no way of assessing how some of the garbage in the Agency file, including anonymous tips or slanders from family or ex-spouses, impact the assessor. The assessor reviews the files from the child's school and from anyone involved with the child on a professional basis. All hospital records and criminal records will be available as well. The assessor considers the medical or mental-health issues of both the parent and the child and any allegations regarding drug or alcohol abuse or anger-management issues. Observations of the child's behavioural issues form a key part of the material in play. In almost all cases, the assessor views parents and children interacting together. Conscientious assessors often interview collateral people, such as workers, doctors or teachers, who can shed light on the issues.

Assume that everything in your life, and your child's life, will get put down, churned up and considered in an assessment. Some of the more obvious issues that an assessment will address include family dynamics, parenting skills, physical or sexual abuse of the child and previous physical or sexual abuse of a parent. Emotional abuse is relevant; likewise, so is parental response to past problems.

How the assessment comes about

As indicated, when the Agency has concerns about the child-caring abilities of a parent, they usually request an assessment in a nonconfrontational way first, sometimes suggesting or implying that it is the parent's opportunity to prove the Agency wrong and demonstrate that they do, in fact, have sufficient parenting skills to raise these children. If the parents fail to consent to an assessment, the Agency may ask the court to order one.

When to consent

Generally, if the Agency felt you possessed sufficient parenting skills to deal with a child, they wouldn't be seeking an assessment, and if they possessed a slam-dunk case without an assessment, they wouldn't want to pay for one. When the Agency agrees to pay for a Parenting Capacity Assessment, they usually do so because it results in evidence they need. In fact, almost all parents who submit to an assessment perform poorly—some very poorly—and the assessment turns into a key ingredient in the Agency's case. Even worse, at trial an experienced, court-tested assessor turns into a formidable weapon for the Society. As a rule of thumb, if you receive a poor assessment, you will probably lose at trial. The assessor's evidence will raise serious concerns with the trial judge, sliding him or her toward the Agency's position.

With the above in mind, the decision whether to consent to a Parental Capacity Assessment becomes one of primary importance. Sometimes there are dreadful consequences. It is, in fact, one of the more important issues that you should address with an experienced lawyer. To repeat, *the great majority of assessments find the parents' skills lacking*—usually seriously lacking—and inadequate for the child's needs. In most geographical areas, only a limited number of professionals conduct these assessments, and an assessor is usually chosen from the list of those available to conduct an assessment on a timely basis. The Agency typically puts forth a few names, and it's a reasonable assumption that those assessors have rendered decisions that satisfied the Agency in the past. This is not to suggest that these assessors possess biases in the Agency's favour. In actual fact, a great many of the assessments performed concern parents of limited skills or children with serious problems that pose great challenges to parenting. Nonetheless, it is a given that the Agency does pay for almost all assessments and will have weeded out any assessor who routinely finds in favour of parents.

Against this practical reality set this backdrop: most experts in this area (but not all) consider their duty, expressly or implied, to be owed to the child, with any duty owed to a parent or agency taking a back seat in actual practice. Assessors suffer somewhat, of course, from the curse of the protection case, as do other professionals in the area. An assessor may have endorsed a plan of care that resulted in dire consequences to a child, and any such tragedy may affect his or her subsequent decisions, intentionally or otherwise. While the outcome of an assessment may surprise the Agency on occasion, in most cases it does not. Before the Agency agrees to pay for an assessment, the worker (with his or her university degree[s]), with input from his or her supervisor (ditto) and perhaps other staff members (with their ditto, ditto) assesses the child's needs and the parents' skills, so the decision to proceed with the assessment from the Agency's point of view is based on professional opinion and experience.

Before you consent to an assessment, you must honestly address the basic issues under consideration, and this includes, at the very least, the issues set out below. If the matter proceeds to trial, with or without an assessment, the questions below generally frame what will arise during the course of a protection trial. These concerns become front and centre among the issues raised in an assessment. An experienced lawyer will review these issues with you and offer an assessment of your chances based on his or her reading of the file.

Assessment flaws

I possess an abiding faith in and doglike affection for family-law judges. These folk do not mirror perfection on any level, but they are simply the best option. Seldom is their end of the equation, or system, under attack. Certainly, given the grisly nature and conflicting evidence plopped in front of them, some flunk an occasional case. But I have never appeared in front of a family-court judge in a protection case who did not try to do right by the child. Not once. These people make the entire system work. You want an expert—a family-court judge is an expert. I want *a family-court judge* to make the decision about whether this child should go into care, not someone with charts and questionnaires and tests who is unable to peer into people's hearts and unable to quantify love between a parent and a child. I prefer to throw my clients on the stand and hear them talk about the child's needs and how they will address them. Assessments are complicated, but I have never reviewed one that purported to measure love. In Tuktoyaktuk, I attended the court as a professional legal yapper, a distinguished member of the Harvard Law case-review system, who was mostly ignored, to good result. But in protection cases, the clinical psychologist usually remains just a yapper as well. Cue camera and focus close in on the beleaguered family-court justice who is making serious judgment calls, day in and day out. Sweat pours off her face; the youth of Canada are in her hands. What in hell does she do? Well, here's my guess: she bears down and "mans up." She makes the system work as well as it does. The failures of the system cannot be roped around her neck—individual cases maybe, but not the system. The above comments suggest that most parents should not consent to an assessment. For those who do consent, the observations below outline what a typical assessment purports to address.

Physical care of the child

The first issue examines the physical care of the child. Have you been able to keep the child safe? Has your conduct or that of your spouse resulted in injury to the child? Have you exposed the child to abuse from any other source? Here's a closely related issue: Do you assume responsibility for protecting your child from any potential risks? This includes projected risks that come into play as the child matures.

Emotional care of the child

Have you reinforced and contributed to the emotional development of the child? Have you contributed to the child's self-esteem and emotional development by both encouraging him or her and providing an appropriate role model?

Has your child bonded?

Has the child bonded with you? Starting from infancy, your child should have bonded with you and progressed to bonding with others, forming appropriate relationships that provide a full range of emotional nourishment.

Parenting attitude

Do you have an appropriate attitude toward parenting? Have you acquired proper views about discipline and goals for the child, and have you established proper limits for the child?

Acknowledging problems

Do you acknowledge the child's problems? If serious allegations exist, for instance, about the child's behaviour, and the assessor concludes that these concerns are valid, will they perceive you as being in denial? If so, the assessment would certainly result in a negative conclusion about your parenting skills.

Your feelings toward the child

Any assessment addresses your feelings toward the child. Feelings of resentment or of anger will certainly surface in any assessment, whether you acknowledge those feelings or not. While such feelings exist on some level with all parents, in your case, do they result in inappropriate parenting efforts concerning the child?

Relating to your child

Your compassion or sensitivity toward your child is also an issue addressed in the assessment. While most parents feel that they relate intuitively to their child, an objective assessment may conclude otherwise. A somewhat related issue is your view of the child; namely, do you view the child as a separate person whose wants and desires exist independent of yours? And of course, are you prepared to put your child's interests above your own? This is a fundamental question on many levels.

Parent's background

There are many issues that assessors feel are relevant to an assessment, even though they may not be significant enough to determine the issues involved. Most assessors will seek to examine the background of individual parents and their relationship to each other in order to provide context to their parenting skills. Do you have good or bad memories of experiences with your own parents? If they are bad, can you rise above the memories? Is the relationship between the proposed caregiver spouses (normally the parents) positive? Is the family relationship dysfunctional? Can you resolve your issues in a manner that allows you to parent effectively? In fact, all aspects of family relations provide fodder for the assessment, and an honest evaluation before you engage in an assessment is very important.

Where the child fits in

The above issues are background, to some degree, and may not affect the child directly, but the child's relationship to the family is an important consideration. How does the child actually fit into the family dynamics and interact with you and with his or her siblings? Does your child trust the caregivers? Does the child have a feeling of comfort and security in the home and within the family?

The history of addressing issues

Previous contacts with professionals, including the Agency, will be a relevant factor that the assessor considers. All previous reports or assessments will be made available to the assessor. While the assessor will not necessarily adopt the conclusions of previous professionals, he or she will place a considerable emphasis on your willingness to accept guidance from those professionals.

In many protection cases, an adversarial relationship has already developed between the parents and the Agency at this stage, and unfortunately, this may affect the results of the assessment. Unwillingness to change or accept change on the part of the parents is often a key factor in assessments that find ongoing problems with the children. Can you set aside your personal attitudes for the sake of the children and work with service providers? On the same note, can you benefit from the sort of help that the assessor thinks is needed? You can expect that a history of seeking help without following through will form part of the assessor's consideration, but a past willingness to seek help with some success will count in your favour.

What happens if you refuse to be assessed

Some parents refuse to be assessed. What happens if you do not participate in an assessment after the court orders it? In most jurisdictions, the court will draw an *adverse inference* against you, meaning they may infer that you would not have done well or even that you would have fared poorly in an assessment. This adverse inference normally arises at trial. In some cases, the inference may be far preferable to having an expert give you a horrendous assessment. In the former situation, you still have the option of putting your story directly to the trial judge and refuting that inference.

Arriving at this decision involves careful, objective weighing of the issues raised above and of the probable results of an assessment. You may decide that taking the witness stand and addressing the issues raised above, through your own testimony, is the best course of action—but such a decision is fraught with peril. Many well-intentioned parents simply do not do well on the witness stand. Involve an experienced lawyer or a qualified professional such as a psychologist in the decision to provide an opinion on the issues raised and the available options. A bad Parenting Capacity Assessment, however, remains very difficult to overcome at trial, with or without counsel. And it often puts the issue of whether your child is in need of protection into the hands of a psychologist, when the best person to assess protection issues may in fact be the trial judge.

Chapter 7

Matters after Temporary Care but before Trial

After resolution of the issue of temporary care, when the court probably ordered the child to remain in care for the time being, other issues arise that a parent should address. These are the matters that will help you advance your case if it proceeds to trial and that will perhaps allow you to resolve the matter before trial.

Lawyer for the child

In most jurisdictions, a normally functioning 12-year-old has a lawyer appointed to place the child's wishes before the court. When there are siblings in care who are approaching that age, the court may request that the lawyer also put their wishes before the court. The age limit for this is flexible, so that a mature 10-year-old might have his or her wishes accommodated, while a child older than the age of 12 with mental-health issues might not. Very often, the lawyer for the child is appointed at the first or second return of the matter, but this is not always the case, and you may wish to ask the court for such an appointment.

Disclosure

A parent involved in child-protection proceedings possesses the right to disclosure of the Agency's file to examine the case against him or her. To obtain disclosure, you can contact the appropriate person in the Agency and make an appointment to see the file and then wade through the 8 to 15 inches of material that they typically possess. The only things you may not be entitled to view are matters covered by *privilege*—such things as communications between the Agency and its lawyer. A prudent parent lists the documents produced at disclosure. Documents produced at trial and not previously disclosed to you would warrant an objection from you. The worker's (or workers') notes probably stand as the most important item in the Society's file—except perhaps for any expert reports concerning the child. You should obtain a copy of the worker's notes from the Agency, and if they fail to provide you with a copy, ask the judge for them. These notes assist in preparing cross-examination for trial.

Examining or questioning the Agency worker

Following disclosure of the Agency's file, you get a turn to question or examine the worker under oath. The first order of business at the questioning (or cross-examination) of this witness is to establish his or her background and credentials. If he or she does not produce a resume, start your questioning with what the worker did after high school (perhaps the first question would be, "Did you graduate high school?"), and continue to ask simple questions that lead the worker through his or her education from that point, including programs, courses taken and detailed substantive content of all courses relevant to the job or to the case. Question the worker with respect to all past employment and all experience, in detail, relevant to his or her job or the case. Question the worker with respect to special interests or hobbies. He or she may, for instance, have a hobby that involves working with special-needs kids, and this experience may turn out to be relevant. If you learn of this fact only at trial, you may be at a disadvantage if it plays into the trial issues. Very often, the worker will produce his or her resume. Make it an exhibit at the questioning. And question the worker about every item in the resume.

After questioning the worker about his or her credentials, an easy way to cover the appropriate issues in the Agency file is as follows:

Q. *When did the Agency first become involved with this file?*

Q. *What was the next contact noted in the file?*

Q. *What was the next contact noted in the file?*

At this point, all you have to do is keep repeating this question until the Agency case has been set out in full. When this examination is complete, the parent should have the crux of the Agency's file set out in detail, under oath. Order a copy of the transcript. You will need to order a copy for the judge if you intend to use it at trial.

This transcript can be used at trial to assist in the cross-examination of the worker, to ensure that his or her story remains consistent. In a case where there has been more than one Agency worker involved in the file, the parent may request that these additional workers also be produced for examination. An observation: the purpose of this examination is to advance your case—not to vent on or admonish the worker.

Motions

One of the primary ways a lawyer advances a case is through motions, and a motion is not so complicated an affair that you can't avail yourself of the same opportunity. In lay terms, as previously indicated, a motion is simply a request you make of a judge. For instance, it may be a request that you be allowed more access to the child or that you be allowed to examine the police records of someone involved. A motion is usually a temporary request, made to push the case along, as opposed to resolving it on a final basis. A motion, as noted above, is *supported*; that is, backed up by a sworn statement (affidavit) made by a person with knowledge of the facts set out.

A party may file multiple affidavits in support of a motion, where appropriate. As noted, motions are brought on temporary issues. They normally do not resolve the matter in full but are brought to assist in resolution of a matter and, often, to assist a party if the matter proceeds to trial. Common motions in protection matters may be as follows: a motion to have a lawyer appointed for the child; a motion to question a witness; a motion for a Parenting Capacity Assessment or a motion to force the Agency to produce certain documents.

Developing or refining a plan of care

It is probably never too late to develop or refine a plan of care to present to the court at trial. Regardless of where you sit in the court process, setting out a proper plan of care for the child is a must in every situation. Again, if the time draws near to trial and no family or other acceptable supports materialize, it may be prudent to develop contacts with local community or church groups. As noted elsewhere, a proper plan of care dispels concerns that a court has in placing the child with you. A strong plan addresses, and hopefully eliminates, all the concerns a court would have. Many churches offer counselling or programs a parent can use, and some of the more proactive ones may involve themselves in your plan of care, perhaps as backup, to transport children or even for day-to-day involvement to address issues. As noted, judges return children when they feel a comfort level about the proposed care of the child.

Generally, preparing for trial

Preparation for trial in a child-protection matter involves addressing the issues raised by the Agency, either by preparing to refute their allegations or by addressing the root causes and correcting those problems. Was your child exposed to an inappropriate caregiver, an abusive spouse or a parent with drug or alcohol issues? If the allegations are accurate, or if they appear to be accurate, address these issues well before trial, so you can take as many issues as possible off the table before trial. If the allegations involve anger management, the answer is for you to attend anger management programs and collect the diplomas or certificates. But beware—if you simply sit in a remedial program and refuse to engage, you will likely face the program director or counsellor at the trial while they testify about your lack of involvement in the program. This principle applies to any remedial program that you have undertaken, including parenting courses or programs for alcohol or drug abuse. Do not skip classes and participate like hell. In addition, make sure the program director knows your name and understands your commitment to the program. Some programs recommend repeat programs or subsequent courses. Know what is expected of you with respect to each allegation, and understand what will realistically satisfy the Agency's concerns in the eyes of the court.

If you are a young or underage mom seeking the return of your child, you should carefully review the options the Agency has presented. The Agency probably can arrange for a teaching placement, in which you will enter a residential program and be coached by experienced mothers and counsellors about child care and development. The Agency does not possess an unlimited supply of such placements, so when they offer one, it telegraphs that the Agency conceals no hidden agenda, except to see you learn how to care for your child properly. Most lawyers in the child-protection area endorse such a placement and would counsel you to accept the opportunity.

In a great percentage of protection cases, the parents should seek out the advice and assistance of experts in the community to provide opinions at trial that address the issues in play. While there are multiple avenues for therapy available in most communities, other experts may be harder to locate. If you need an expert for a complicated technical matter, requiring perhaps university credentials or even medical credentials, haunt university psychiatric, psychological or medical faculties or schools online for names, contact numbers or references—and pursue these options aggressively. Very often, experts are available to review your case and help you, for reasonable sums or on a pro bono basis. However, I have never personally encountered a pro bono expert, and the species may well be extinct.

The time trap

Time in a protection case often poses traps for the unwary. When the Agency seeks an order over a child for six months, for example, this period does not normally start to run until the judge signs the order. It is not backdated to the time of apprehension. So if your child was apprehended, and if there are four months of negotiations until you and Agency come to agreement, it could result in your child being in care for 10 months. But if the matter remains in dispute and goes to trial, the child may face one year, or possibly even two years, in care before the matter is resolved. And the Agency will rightly raise this *time* argument with you, trying to force early resolution.

Agreed statements

Most cases are resolved short of trial, by agreement. This agreement sets out the facts—essentially what you did wrong plus how you propose to address those problems. Some parents will agree and sign documents or statements that are false in material respects just to have their children returned or to minimize the time the children spend in care. This presents a problem if the matter returns to court in the future, as the earlier document will be used against you, and whatever you signed will become part of the second court case. This situation is a common occurrence in protection cases. Most parents will say or do anything to have their children returned, including signing pieces of paper containing falsehoods. Subsequent courts, however, will not be receptive to a repudiation of the original agreement. You signed it, it binds you—no matter that it might have been signed out of love for the child. No matter. This should make a parent pause and consider well before signing off in the first court case.

Here is a plea to family-court judges: acknowledge that good parents in this situation would crawl through hellfire on their hands and knees to have their child returned, so consenting to a few erroneous facts in these agreements should be taken with a grain of salt. Drop the hard-ass pose when considering previously agreed statements and recall that the bottom-line purpose of the process is to address the child's situation, not previous pieces of paper obtained under duress.

Chapter 8

Mental Health, Disabilities
and the System

Mental health

Mental-health issues abound in protection proceedings. Thousands of cases involve children with mental-health issues and mystified, even terrified, parents. Thousands more involve parents with mental-health issues and confused or traumatized children, and all cases allege that the children are at risk. Yes, it often appears as if all the nut factories in the world have worked overtime to burden the child-protection systems in Canada. Sadly, there is no nut-fairy to fly to the rescue. The skill with which mental-health issues are addressed in protection matters varies dramatically from case to case, jurisdiction to jurisdiction and court to court.

One of the more tragic situations facing lawyers in this area is the struggling (perhaps single) parent with a special-needs child who herself has mental-health issues. In many cases, the parent's lack of professional skills and insufficient or inappropriate responses only serve to worsen the child's behaviour problems. The parent, having struggled with these behaviours for months or even years, now faces allegations that the behaviour problems result solely from poor parenting. Such a suggestion often starts or widens the rift between the parents and the worker. From the worker's viewpoint, all he or she sees is a parent not dealing appropriately with a child who is out of control.

On the other side of the coin, there may be a parent who is overwhelmed or has mental-health issues. The parent may have a fair grasp of reality but maybe not quite enough to keep a relatively normal child from becoming "hell on wheels." In both of these somewhat typical situations, diverting extensive community-health resources to the family on a timely basis could have kept this family and child out of the legal system. Sadly, these community resources are not always available; the Agency possesses limited resources and is not particularly set up to deal with mental-health issues, among others. As noted, front-line Agency workers face hostile parents on a regular basis and usually assume the worst, for the child's sake. The above situations definitely reveal protection issues. Young workers may not understand family dynamics as well as more experienced workers, so they will focus on protection above all else. Their training emphasizes and reemphasizes protection issues.

And of course, there are workers, and then there are workers. Some workers respond better to different types of problems. Some can keep the above situations out of court, often for some time, but eventually the workers will rotate, and the family scenarios outlined above will derail, the protection issues will escalate and a mental-health problem will wind up on a court list.

Physical disabilities or disease

In somewhat rarer situations, similar results arise when a physical disability or serious disease presents a protection issue. The striking difference in these cases is that the worker is not usually called upon to make judgment calls about the nature of the risk. Health-care providers have probably already diagnosed the problem and suggested treatment plans. And of course there is no stigma to having a child or parent with cancer, for example, while mental-health issues presenting in a child will raise immediate, sometimes unwarranted, assumptions about the nature of the problem and the risks involved.

The system

Lawyers are sometimes chagrined when they leave a courtroom after the hearing of a contested matter in which the justice accurately digested and correctly interpreted mounds of often-conflicting material—only to have the client rail against the system because the justice indicated that the child was 6 years old rather than 5 or missed some other equally irrelevant point.

A parent expects and demands justice. In each case that comes before it, the court is routinely expected to understand all issues—whether legal, medical, societal or personal—and to review and fully digest each report, to memorize all the pleadings and affidavit material and to intuitively assess the parents' abilities and children's needs. The same judge, of course, faces the same demands in dealing with the next 15 cases on the docket.

In higher courts or appeal courts, and in other jurisdictions, the system sometimes directs that a judge be chosen from a panel of certain justices with particular expertise to hear certain types of cases, so that a judge with a background in, say, bankruptcy law, is directed to those types of cases rather than, say, a multijurisdictional anti-combines case. But judges who hear protection cases, except in a situation in which they recuse (withdraw) themselves from a case, must hear whatever comes before them. A justice may have a Monday court case dealing with a child with ADHD and an argument about what the best treatment program is; on Tuesday, a case with alleged trauma to an unborn child; on Wednesday, a case about whether a child with learning disabilities is adoptable; a Thursday case about the degree to which parents can impose religious preferences to limit a child's schooling and on Friday, the justice may have to decide whether an abusive parent has reformed, in order to assess the present risk to the child. In addition to everything else, justices are expected to be authorities on mental-health issues, an area of human life that is witnessing rapid treatment advances.

If your case involves mental-health issues, I advise you to gain a firm understanding of the basic principles of mental-health treatment options. This understanding should precede developing a strategy in the case and drafting an Answer and Plan of Care. In order to effectively advance your case, a plan of care involving mental-health issues may have to educate at the same time: "I have been diagnosed by xxx as xxx. Dr. xxx, my psychiatrist, advises me that xxx is a drug that treats this disorder, and I have been taking the meds on prescription since xxx. I have also been taking counselling to help me with xxx."

Understanding the mental-health issues in a case remains fundamental to discerning whether the court and the treating professionals are on the same page when the matter heads toward trial. The lead professional in many mental-health cases should be a psychiatrist, but for many reasons it may be a clinical psychologist, a professional not normally entitled to prescribe medications—an issue that may come into play. If severe psychiatric issues are involved, either with respect to the child or one of the parents, you need a psychiatrist in your corner.

The role of medication

Obviously, bodies and brains include a seemingly endless variety of emotional and mental states. They often fail to function with perfection, and medications can address many health issues. Nonetheless, there are people who adamantly refuse all medications, for themselves and their children. Sometimes this is for religious reasons, sometimes for moral reasons, and sometimes just because they are ornery. Advancing a protection case successfully often involves giving weight to the majority view on any issue. Lawyers often face situations in which the child has been labelled ADHD, or something similar, and has been prescribed medication, perhaps because the teacher has complained that the child will not or cannot pay attention in class. The behaviour of the child in the classroom often triggers Agency involvement. "But he's a zombie when on meds," the parents often argue. "He pays attention to me at home and has no problem understanding the material when I explain it to him."

The Agency's position may be that the quiet home atmosphere and the one-on-one attention are what results in the child learning so well. But, indeed, it may well be the fault of an unsympathetic or overworked teacher. But parents who refuse to medicate in accordance with the accepted view run the risk of Agency involvement. Hell, if life were easy, no one would waste money on lottery tickets.

Sadly for those people who disagree with all medication on principle, the diagnosis and treatment of mental-health issues in the past 20 years has led to the inescapable conclusion that many of these illnesses have a biological component susceptible to treatment by way of meds. This is not to suggest that medication alone will necessarily address protection cases adequately. Most courts, even when confronted with a proper diagnosis and prescription by a psychiatrist, would cast a jaundiced eye if there were no appropriate therapy included to address serious past issues at the same time.

If you wish a court to buy into your proposed plan of care, it may involve accepting or accommodating conventional wisdom in the plan. Medication alone may solve some problems. Psychotherapy may solve some problems; visits to a priest or minister, or wise aunt, or a shaman may solve some problems; and some, admittedly not too many, may be cured by just standing in the rain. However, placing a plan before a court should carry as its primary purpose the return of the children to the people proposing that plan, rather than pushing the proposed caregivers' views on any particular issue. Mental-health issues have a biological component, but there is also a clear role for a sympathetic therapist, and a plan of care should address both sides of this equation as set out below.

The family doctor and court

Alarm bells should sound if your plan depends solely upon your family doctor to present your side of a case when heavy-duty mental health issues are involved. The family doctor normally is not an expert in the diagnosis of psychiatric disorders, of the medications involved in their treatment or the appropriate therapy needed to address related issues. The family doctor does not usually present an acceptable alternative to the appropriate expert. Certainly, lacking any other evidence, the opinion of a family doctor is relevant, but beware of situations where other expert evidence contradicts the doctor's opinion.

Juvenile bipolar disorder

Children with juvenile bipolar disorder often present challenges on many levels. When parents or grandparents are afflicted with bipolar disorder, and the children in question are exhibiting odd, even bizarre behaviour, a visit to the Juvenile Bipolar Research Foundation website may offer clues about diagnosis and treatment. These children are often misdiagnosed with depression, ADHD (attention deficit hyperactivity disorder), oppositional defiant disorder or OCD (obsessive-compulsive disorder).

The meds plus the therapy

The best trial judges, as noted previously, are those callus-butted jurists who over the years have acquired the ability to read witnesses accurately, to sift through contradictory testimony and evidence and to assess the facts and people correctly. The ability to synthesize expert testimony, however, is a different skill, which often requires a proper grounding or understanding of the area in question. Incorrect or dated ideas about mental-health issues abound in everyone, including judges. The development of diagnostic tools and drug therapies has advanced and continues to advance so rapidly that busy courts have difficulty keeping abreast. As noted, a plan of care involving mental-health issues should assume that the reader of that plan has little grounding in the theoretical or practical aspects of mental health.

The new-generation of selective serotonin-reuptake inhibitors (SSRIs), namely Prozac, Zoloft and Paxil, can address the afflictions of depression and obsessive-compulsive disorder. Anxiety can often be treated by diazepam and alprazolam, panic disorder with Xanax, and bipolar disorder with lithium and Seroquel. Those suffering from hallucinatory disorders often find relief with Thorazine and other antipsychotic drugs. But there is no guarantee that simply indicating that the illness has been diagnosed and the prescription filled will address the protection concerns adequately. The foregoing treatments can all be bolstered by a plan that uses therapy in addition to the drugs. While prescription medications possess their resident boosters and naysayers, few would argue that proper therapy harms any plan. One may debate the individual type of therapy, whether cognitive behavioural, psychodynamic or interpersonal, but a therapeutic intervention by a sympathetic therapist, coupled with a proper drug regime, will advance the majority of cases in which mental-health issues give rise to protection concerns.

Chapter 9

Addictions

Alcohol dependency has always been a problem in the child-protection field, but drug addiction now equals or exceeds it as a concern. In addition to drug and alcohol addictions, courts now also recognize a gambling addiction as possibly raising protection concerns. Can addiction to knitting or candy floss be far behind? Protection cases abound with references to residential programs, treatment facilities, testing centres, and counselling programs that didn't exist in past years, and enrolling and completing these plans is almost mandatory when addictions lead to the concerns.

The culture

In addiction situations, a "culture" often accompanies, and this telegraphs a message to the Agency. An alcohol problem might involve the same group of friends throwing eight or nine cases of beer in a pickup truck every Friday night or two sisters sipping sherry every afternoon. Or it might be a couple that the police are called to deal with on a regular basis. In the case of drugs, the culture may involve associating with known users, or it may involve criminal activity to support the addiction: a history of petty property crimes, inability to meet rent payments or incidents of prostitution. The culture for gambling addictions might involve reckless borrowing, minor thefts or families left without the necessities.

Experienced judges can identify a troubling culture, even if there is no empirical evidence of the addiction. So when you address the addiction, address the culture at the same time. This can be an easy, early way of indicating to the Agency or to the court that you have addressed the relevant protection issues.

Alcohol

When alcohol becomes an issue in a protection case, nothing less than abstinence and involvement in a recognized program, along with random and periodic testing, satisfies the court. The suggestion that a parent with problems can now use alcohol wisely is a difficult concept to sell, and relying on this principle is fraught with peril when your children are involved in a protection case. In a nutshell: if you are involved in a child-protection case and the allegations involve alcohol, you need to enrol in a recognized program and submit to random testing. The subtleties of any other approach will probably not wash.

Drugs

Allegations of drug use by the proposed caregiver carry a far more onerous burden in practice than do alcohol allegations. While most courts can empathize with a parent who drinks too much and succumbs to problems with liquor, few possess any tolerance for drug addiction. Courts retain a healthy scepticism about plans advanced by caregivers when allegations of drug abuse have been made. Accordingly, the obvious answer to this allegation is a plan that safeguards the child, coupled with regular and random urine testing or (increasingly frequent) hair-follicle testing. Until the drug testing is in place and the proof available, you may be well advised to place the children with other family members.

Testing

Testing for drugs or alcohol invariably involves assessing many variables—variables particular to both the suspected user and the substance for which the user is being tested. Testing labs are available in all major centres.

Parents should note that the principles of testing that apply in child-protection cases may be different than in other areas. Except in situations in which safety is an issue, when alcoholism is a concern in the workplace, random drug testing may affect the rights of the employee and raise a human-rights argument—but there is little court support for applying this principle to protection situations.

Follicle testing

Hair-follicle analysis tests the toxins that have been deposited in the hair. The toxins are trapped inside the hair and remain there until the hair is cut. Hair grows at approximately half an inch per month, so head-hair testing generally has approximately a 90-day window of time, but body hair testing may disclose toxins for the past year. Normally, the part of the hair that was close to the scalp will be tested. The toxins or substances tested for can include cocaine (cocaine and benzoylecgonine), marijuana, opiates (codeine, morphine, and 6-monacteyl morphine), methamphetamine (methamphetamine/amphetamine and ecstasy) and phencyclidine (PCP).

Alcohol abuse

The chemical substance in alcohol that is addictive is ethanol or ethyl alcohol, and one can measure its presence in the body with a Breathalyzer or by testing blood, saliva or urine. The type of testing sought in protection cases could include both urinalysis and follicle testing, depending upon the allegations.

Addressing drug allegations, as noted, involves placing the child in a situation of safety and pursuing programs and testing. If alcohol is involved, the plan is similar. It goes without saying that a program of therapy to combat any addiction will succeed only if the participant has the requisite will.

Some programs have higher success rates than others do and may carry more credibility with the courts. The Alcoholics Anonymous program bears special mention in this regard. This program has a much higher success rate than many other programs, and the nature of the program is such that participants must signal a willingness to address past behaviour. The drug disulfiram, sold under the trade name Antabuse, is a medication that gives takers a severe, immediate reaction to alcohol. It has success rates of approximately 50 percent.

Chapter 10

The Abusive Parent Forced to Bail

One somewhat typical protection situation deserves consideration because it occurs more often than you might think. It might happen this way: following involvement with the family, the Agency worker focuses on one parent, usually the male, as the root of all evil in the family. This situation often involves an abusive male spouse, who demonstrates a controlling personality as well, coupled with a somewhat submissive spouse and young children in the home.

At the lawyer's office

At some point, often before court has been scheduled but occasionally after it has started, both spouses attend the lawyer's office and minimize the abuse or deny the situation entirely; they then often request a joint defence. The obvious issue in legal representation crystallizes, namely that if the parties' positions change in the future and they then develop opposing interests, the lawyer cannot act for either—resulting in delay and possibly confusion, which is sometimes a serious problem in itself in protection cases. But in addition to considering that potential problem, parents should honestly reevaluate their positions in light of the following possible developments.

Children in a home with abuse

From a protection point of view, this issue is of concern because of the presence of children in an abusive relationship. The suggestion that the abusive relationship between adults does not affect the children is patently untenable, even where the children themselves are not being abused. To the worker, the solution in this type of situation is crystal clear: get rid of the abusive spouse. But there is no litmus test to establish whether the children are better off with the father in the family, with all this implies, or whether they would be better off if the father were ostracized from the family, with all but minimal contact. While an abusive relationship is not to be condoned, the issue in theory remains: What is in the best interests of the child? Nevertheless, the Agency's position will no doubt be that removing the father is best for the children, a concept that will not be tested fully until trial. By that time, it is unlikely that any weight will be given to an alternative proposal.

At the Temporary-Care hearing, the Agency in these cases will not likely consider any alternative wherein the father remains in the home. To avoid an apprehension, the father often departs from the scene. However, the problem can escalate from that point, if the home was one where the father was key to maintaining a functioning household. If there are sufficient supports available to the mother and proper assistance from the Agency, a subsequent apprehension may be avoided. But if the family flounders, it is unlikely the Agency will consent to reintroducing the father to the family, short of trial.

After a Temporary-Care hearing in which the court refuses to let the father into the home and prohibits him from contacting the family, the situation often results in subterfuge by the parents. The father, having left the home, may engage in furtive visits to the family, placing all of them in a difficult position. If the mother is discovered lying to or misleading the Agency, the family will be court-bound once more, with the children likely heading for foster care. In some situations, older children are coerced into lying to the worker, with the same likely result. Any confirmed sighting of the father with the family, even if they are just shopping for food or staples, could conceivably result in an apprehension but in any event would be viewed with suspicion.

A possible strategy

Once the Agency is involved in a situation similar to that described above, it is a recipe for steady, sometimes rapid, deterioration. One way to forestall this involves an early assessment of the situation and a blunt acknowledgement of the problem by the abusive spouse. Resolution will involve an immediate mea culpa, coupled with promises (and with follow-through) to take recommended courses and counselling and to a make a serious effort to address the worker's immediate concerns. These cases rarely resolve in this way, however.

Chapter 11

The Trial

Bear in mind the following fact: most self-represented people do poorly in court. Since the future welfare of your child is at stake, the advice to every parent in a protection case, once again, is to make every effort to obtain legal counsel rather than representing yourself. This book will neither replace nor be equal to having an experienced lawyer on your side in any court proceeding.

While parents should always have a lawyer representing them at trial, sometimes they do not. Conducting a trial involves skills that may improve with practice, and even though the following sections are set out in lay terms and with the self-represented person in mind, applying these principles properly in any given situation is far from easy, even for legal counsel. But the point to bear in mind is this: the only goal at trial is to give the judge a comfort level in regard to the care of your child.

Trial Prep 101

Proper preparation for any trial, including a protection trial, involves a substantial amount of work, mostly work done well in advance. The issues that come up in a trial are somewhat predictable, and a reasonably intelligent parent should be able to understand the issues. Self-represented people have a right to their day in court and a right to present their case and make submissions to the court about the issues in play. And in my experience, they have a right to kiss the child good-bye at the end of the trial.

Visit the courthouse before the trial

If you haven't been to the courthouse and the trial date is approaching, you should take a trip there and sit in on some matrimonial proceedings. Protection courts remain closed to the public, but family courts do not. Provincial or territorial family-court proceedings will help you get a general feel for the atmosphere, see where people sit, learn when to stand up and sit down and see how the proceedings are conducted.

Documents before trial

Protection cases start with the filing of documents in court by the Agency, and time limits govern the filing of answering material by the parents. If you fail to file your answer on time, you may not be able to participate in the court process thereafter. Once those documents are filed, however, the documentation required to get to trial is somewhat minimal, and most judges are usually lenient toward self-represented people. The rules in every jurisdiction provide for the filing of certain material before trial; the purpose is to avoid surprise at trial, and you would be prudent to remember that basic rule. Few lay people would sort through the documents to be filed for trial, but it probably wouldn't be fatal. Courts will normally still wish to hear both sides of the story before making a decision about the children, and they would expect the Agency lawyer to see that all relevant documents have been filed or are available for filing. Most Agency lawyers are diligent in that regard.

Before the trial, perhaps even on the first day of trial, the Agency lawyer may ask you to consent to certain documents being filed with the court. Sometimes they want the documents filed merely to push the procedure along, but sometimes the documents push their case and hurt yours. Unless the ramifications of filing those documents are crystal clear to you, you should politely decline. The stakes, after all, are quite high. While a court will expect a lawyer to know which documents it is appropriate to consent to, the bar for an unrepresented parent is somewhat lower. Some of these documents are rather routine, and some are not. If there is anything in the documents that you take issue with, politely decline to consent to the filing. The lawyer has other options available. You may face some heat from the Agency lawyer over this decision.

The media illusion

Courtroom battles loom as a staple of prime-time television. Images invariably show articulate, well-dressed lawyers gesturing madly, riveting a judge and jury with brilliant argument and winning the day. Obviously, this is an exaggeration in so many ways, not the least of which follows. In Canadian protection cases, there is no jury; a judge is always the ultimate trier of fact. Good courtroom lawyers are seldom eloquent; they just work like dogs. If they are flamboyantly dressed, it is an accident, perhaps the result of a daring spouse, as most lawyers strive to look professional only. Brilliant dialogue remains on the TV screen alone. Discourse in a trial is usually without exaggeration and rather pointed. Judges want to hear relevant discussion or receive evidence far more than they wish to receive fanciful theories or extravagant argument. The judge listens to the allegations of the Agency, assesses the risk, and listens carefully to your response. He or she has to decide: Is the child at risk? Or have you addressed that risk? Ultimately, can you keep this child from harm?

Some observations about dress

Courtrooms possess dress codes, even though no one may mention it to you. Dress neatly. If possible, men should wear a dark suit or perhaps a sports coat, a light-coloured shirt and a tie. Women should wear a dark blazer, dark skirt and light-coloured blouse. If you don't own this apparel, just keep it neat. No cleavage for women, and preferably no bare arms for anyone. Nobody awards points for visible tattoos or body rings, and remember that gum chewing or the wearing of a hat will normally bring a rebuke. Once again, dressing appropriately sends a message to the court. Your presence in court indicates that you want something from the judge, and your dress and conduct in court send messages to the judge.

A warning: a judge may be cranky. This does not signify anything. He or she is probably angry at having the fate and future of your child in his or her hands. Often a cranky judge will telegraph concerns early in the proceeding, allowing you to make adjustments to your case—so listen carefully, and think hard about what the judge says and how he or she acts. Many judges try to give everybody something, especially at the motion stage but also after the trial. (Reread the anecdote titled "Tuktoyaktuk" at the beginning of the book.) Ultimately, however, what a judge actually does is more important than what he or she says.

Get to court early on the first day of trial to help overcome any anxiety. (I always tried to throw up four or five times at home before the start of a trial, to spare the court cleaning staff.) Introduce yourself to the court clerk and provide your name to him or her, written in block letters on a piece of paper, so he or she can pass it on to the judge. Courtroom layouts are fairly predictable. The big, high seat belongs to the judge. This is not open for discussion, no matter who gets there first. There will probably be a witness box, in which each witness will sit or stand. There may or not be a chair in the box. If one of your witnesses is older or infirm, you may ask the judge for a chair. The judge never refuses.

Your first order of business is to ask the court clerk where you sit. There are usually two counsel tables, but if there are more than two parties, the clerk or the justice will often have ordered additional tables. If there is no table, and you need one for your papers, ask the clerk to indicate to the judge that you require one. Lawyers are no more entitled to such simple courtesies than you are. Addressing the judge is simple. Refer to him or her as "Your Honour." For instance, "Your Honour, I object to that question . . ."

When to stand and talk

When the judge comes into the room, the court clerk will ask all to rise. Throughout the proceedings, stand when addressing the court, and sit when you are not. If you wish to object to something, for example to evidence that the Agency is trying to introduce, you should stand up, interrupt and say very clearly. "I object, Your Honour," and then wait until the judge asks what the objection is. Courtrooms are intended to be civil places, even though the stakes may be extremely important to you. Don't lose your temper. Take turns with the Agency lawyer when speaking. Displays of temper may make you feel better but rarely help your case. On a somewhat related point, the two most common objections to evidence are "that is irrelevant" and "that is hearsay," but most judges want to hear everything and simply assign less or more weight to the evidence presented.

Surprise

Before trial, there may be some paperwork for the self-represented parent. If you will be relying on documents to prove your case, serve copies of these documents on the other lawyers (or the other parties, if they are representing themselves). As noted earlier, the court expects all parties to disclose the basic points of their case, to avoid "trial by ambush." Once again, there are powerful media images at work that may lead you astray in practice; a prime example is the screen portrayal of a lawyer who presents a surprise document or witness to win the case. Surprises from either party will not impress the judge in a protection trial. To repeat, if you think that surprising the court with a witness or a document will win the day, you should think again. Courts are unanimous in the concept of full disclosure in a protection matter. If you produce a document not provided to the other side beforehand, the court will usually adjourn in fairness to the other party and may even order that you pay the associated costs of the adjournment. There may be exceptions to this concept in cross-examination, but for the most part, courts are sceptical about the ambush theory. To repeat, a big surprise will usually result in an adjournment, with the party who is responsible for the surprise facing an order that they pay costs. So, no surprises, and all cards on the table at all times are the rules of thumb.

Will-say lists

In some jurisdictions, parties are asked to file affidavits for trial for some or all witnesses, outlining their evidence; once again, this is done to avoid surprise. In other jurisdictions, you just produce a list of your witnesses, outlining in brief what that witness will say—to wit, what lawyers call a *will-say* list. For instance, a brief summary (please note that this should be succinct, i.e., highlights only) might say, "John Doe will say that he has been close to the family for 20 years and has never seen the parents hit any of their children." For you, producing a *will-say* list for every one of your witnesses will serve as a focus in putting your case together. When read together, the will-says, including your own, should address all protection issues and, *if believed*, should result in the children being returned to you. These will-says are to assist the judge, to help her understand the case and the issues involved. They are not evidence.

Trial strategy

There are thousands of books on trial strategies for every type of case. Lawyers always have a strategy for each case they take to trial, and they understand and usually prepare this strategy well in advance of the trial. Through witnesses, the Agency will produce a litany of facts in their effort to have the child remain in their care. Every parent involved in a protection matter has been served with the usual amount of Agency material, so you should have a fair idea of what the Society's complaints are. Start with this material and formulate a list of the Agency's complaints. Review the material again, and outline who the likely witnesses for the Society will be and what they will say. Sometimes more than one of their witnesses will address the same complaint, especially when there have been successive workers on the file. Work through the material again and again until you can put together a comprehensive list of the Society's witnesses and have a very close idea of what those witnesses will say. This is the case that you have to meet. This is the case you will have to refute if you wish to have your child returned. This is the issue, or issues, about which you must give the judge a comfort level.

Evidence in general

Lawyers study evidence in law school and polish their understanding of these rules in practice—in theory. It may give you some comfort to know that most lawyers in protection matters have only a cursory knowledge of the rules of evidence. Most know squat. In all probability, the judge knows more evidentiary rules than everyone else in the courtroom combined. But when courts decide the fate of a child, rules of evidence always take second place. Always. The judge seeks a complete understanding of the facts in the case at hand before making any decision, and the facts trump even the niftiest rule of evidence. This somewhat levels the playing field for the self-represented parent. Repeat: no arcane rule of evidence will keep a justice from placing a child with the Agency or from returning that child to the parent. To reiterate: a child-protection proceeding is never won on the basis of a rule of evidence, notwithstanding the fact that the written reason may say so. Rules of evidence are for other courts and TV drama. The bottom line is this: no court lets an obscure rule of evidence decide what happens to a child.

What is "evidence"?

Evidence is just *stuff*, stuff put before the court to assist them in arriving at a decision. Maybe it includes verbal testimony, maybe a report card, maybe a police report, but it's just stuff, both words and pieces of paper. Both sides put this stuff before the court to bolster their positions. In practice, most evidence comes in the form of reports filed or witnesses testifying. It may be an Agency worker who says the parent beat the child, or perhaps it's a parent's Aunt Eloise testifying on behalf of the parents, who says she saw the kids every Sunday afternoon and they displayed great love for their parents.

Relevance

The first rule of all evidence is that it be relevant and material. And this is not a tough test. If it is marginally on point, it passes this test. In fact, very little fails this test, particularly in protection cases. Judges want to see, hear and understand everything. They may decide that a piece of evidence is inadmissible, but not until they see it and understand what the piece of evidence means.

Hearsay

The rule that gets the best press in courtroom drama and that everyone knows is the Rule Against Hearsay. The witness says, "I heard Fred say . . ." Obviously, the next few words out of the witness probably qualify as hearsay evidence. This rule goes back well more than 100 years in jurisprudence, so it is easy to imagine the subtleties that millions of lawyers have wrought to the principle. This is not an effort to reproduce all of those complexities but merely a few notes to put things in perspective. The rule exists because the court wishes to hear from Fred himself what he said, to prevent skulduggery. Yup, skulduggery! And the hearsay-evidence rule applies not only to oral statements but to documents as well. All documents are hearsay. So that police report or report card is also hearsay—but most jurisdictions have rules that allow this type of evidence to go in.

Getting around hearsay

The best way around hearsay is to have Fred come and give evidence. Quite frankly, you want to put the best possible evidence of your case before the court. With documents, have somebody come to court who possesses personal knowledge of the document: "Yes, I am Ms. Doe, and I am a teacher at Whodunit School. That is, in fact, little Johnnie's report card."

In most protection cases, the court will admit almost everything; however, they will decide for themselves how much weight to give to any particular piece of evidence. When you must rely on hearsay evidence as part of your case, you should have someone present to speak to every document, to demonstrate that the evidence in question is, in fact, reliable and should be given serious weight.

When seeking to introduce untraditional material—for instance, texts from online sources, or that catchy article from some New Zealand child-rearing magazine—the chances of having the court accept it improve dramatically if you have provided the material to the other side well in advance of the trial, so they can do their own research on the matter in question. But be warned—courts do not automatically accept this sort of material. It should ideally be put in through an expert witness.

Opinion evidence

As a self-represented parent in a child-protection matter, there are two times that you get to express an opinion for sure: at the start of the trial, when you briefly advise the court about your theory on the case, and at the end, when you are summing up and offering your opinion on the evidence. In between those two situations, the court only wants to hear opinion evidence from "experts." Once a court decides that a witness is an expert, then the witness can give opinion evidence within the area of their expertise. Sometimes everyone agrees that Dr. So-and-So is an expert in, say, broken bones, and then the trial proceeds. When people don't agree, there will be evidence introduced supporting the proposition that the good doctor is an expert, along with evidence against this point of view, and then the court will decide. As a rule of thumb, if the Agency has shelled out good money for a report, they probably figure that they can qualify Dr. So-and-So as an expert. No rule of law says that an expert has to have university degrees or fancy diplomas. Maybe Aunt Betty, who has been raising kids successfully for 25 years and been taking parenting courses along the way, would qualify as an expert in raising kids. The judge has discretion in these matters, and laypersons are routinely qualified as experts in very narrow areas, allowing them to express an opinion in that narrow area.

How the trial proceeds

Perhaps this fact is obvious: when the judge wants the trial to start, it starts. There appear to be no exceptions to this rule. The judge has absolute control over the courtroom and the process, down to and including how low he or she wants the thermostat set. Each judge sets his or her own schedule. Some start at 9:30 a.m., some at 10:00 a.m., some at 2:00 p.m. They all break for lunch, unless on a diet, or on the wagon, but there is no consistency in the time they choose. They try to break between witnesses, but sometimes they break in the middle of testimony, and if they do so, this is another absolute rule: stay away from that witness until that witness goes back on the stand. Sometimes judges break because they have other matters to deal with. So a day in court might involve four hours or six hours, depending on the foregoing, and while all judges want to hear a matter continuously, sometimes a trial will be adjourned for a few days or a few weeks because of the judge's schedule.

The agency starts

In most situations, the Agency presents their evidence first. So all of their witnesses take the stand and give their evidence, one after the other, and when all of their evidence is before the court, then the parents can call their witnesses and produce their evidence. When there are lawyers for all of the parties, the lawyers might agree to break a case up and take witnesses out of order, to accommodate an out-of-town or expert witness, but unless everyone consents, it would be unusual. You are not required to lead (i.e., to present) any of your case until the Agency's case is all before the court and you know the exact case against you.

Each witness takes the witness stand and must take an oath to affirm that they will tell the truth. The Agency lawyer asks each

Agency witness a series of questions, and the questions will be presented to help the witnesses set out their evidence. This testimony is referred to as the *evidence in chief*. The reason for this name has been lost to history. It is, however, very unlikely to have aboriginal connections. You just have to accept and use the name without comment.

You may object to any question put to the witness, and you make that objection in the manner set out above. When the Agency lawyer finishes questioning a witness, the parents may ask that witness about anything the witness said in response to those questions, and this questioning by the parent is referred to as cross-examination. Yes, it can get somewhat angry at times.

When a new witness begins testimony, the first few questions asked are general in nature, to identify the witness but also to give the witness a chance to relax, and the questions are perhaps along the following lines:

> Q. *State your name, please.*
> A. *Jane Doe.*
> Q. *Will you spell that out please, for the record.*

(The court reporter is making a "record" by taking down everything that is said and will need the correct spelling of everyone's name for any transcripts.)

At this point in the examination, you can ask one or two "leading" questions to set the stage for the testimony that follows.

> Q. *You are a nurse, are you not?*

The question is "leading" because it suggests the answer, namely, that the witness is a nurse. With each new witness, the questioner is allowed two or three leading, noncontentious questions, to set the stage for that particular witness.

> Q. *You are employed as a nurse at Stanton General Hospital?*
> A. *Yes.*

> Q. You were on duty the night that Little
>   Jimmie was admitted?
> A. Yes.

Each witness is in the stand for a purpose—to give evidence about something important to the case. When you arrive at this point in the witness's testimony, you must stop asking leading questions, and if the witness is one of the Agency's, this is the point at which you should raise an objection to any question that is leading. ("I object, Your Honour. That question is leading.")

From a parent's point of view, objecting to a leading question is often a waste of time. The judge may agree with you and ask the lawyer to rephrase the question. So you gain little. The issue becomes important when you, rather than the lawyer, are asking questions. An objection that forces you to rephrase a question may disrupt you and interrupt the flow of thought, so you forget where you were going with a witness. The same thing may happen with a junior counsel, as well. It happened to me for years—many years. The following questions are not leading and avoid this issue completely. You should follow this format:

Use what, where, when and how

What happened next? *What* did you see/hear? *What* did you observe?

What did he say then? *What* did he do then?
Where was that? *Where* were you standing?
When was that?
How old are you? *How* did you happen to be there?

Issues on cross-examination

Perhaps the primary reason that parents hire a lawyer is because of perceived ability to advance a case through cross-examination of the Society's witnesses. But in protection trials, very few lawyers actually accomplish this goal. Most lawyers suck at it. *Yup, most lawyers suck at it.* Most lawyers experienced at this sort of cross-examination do not routinely take these types of cases. In cases with the Agency, most important witnesses for the Society are battle-hardened from previous court experiences. Accordingly, when you are engaged in litigation with the Agency and find yourself in trial, *you should concentrate primarily on advancing your own case through your witnesses* and ensure that they properly push or advance your own case. Concessions from the Society's witnesses represent a bonus but should not be expected.

It is almost impossible to master cross-examination without a great deal of experience, and it always requires diligent preparation. Lawyers who excel in cross-examination, and there aren't all that many in protection cases, have spent years in the trenches. As noted, most effective cross-examination is the result of careful preparation beforehand, but some also comes from quick thinking and prompt reaction at the time a witness says something. However, this latter type of expert cross-examination skill is rare, even in experienced lawyers.

Prepare to cross-examine the Agency witnesses by reviewing the mounds of material you have been served with throughout the course of the lawsuit. Many types of cross-examination exist, but the easiest to master is set out below in a straightforward approach. It is one that any intelligent layperson could use with effect; however, as mentioned before, a parent in trial with the Agency should plan on making their case to the judge with their own witnesses rather than thinking they can produce brilliant results by cross-examining battle-hardened witnesses.

Cross-examination to cut adverse testimony

Say, for instance, that the worker observed the mother hitting the child. During cross-examination, marshal positive facts that are not in dispute (and it is important to use facts that are true and that no one will contradict) to lessen the effect of the incident. The purpose is not to dispute as much as it is to minimize the effect of evidence. Perhaps as follows:

> Q. You indicated that you saw the mother hitting little Susie?
>
> A. —
>
> Q. And you only saw this once. And you've been the worker for 10 years and have visited the home six times.
>
> A. —
>
> Q. There's no indication in the Society file that she ever hit Susie before?
>
> A. —
>
> Q. There's no indication in the file that she ever hit anyone before?
>
> A. —
>
> Q. You have no knowledge of any criminal conviction or the mother for assaulting Susie?
>
> A. —
>
> Q. In fact, the witness has no criminal record at all?
>
> A. —
>
> Q. And there's no indication that Susie ever went to the hospital (clinic, family doctor, etc.)? No indication that neighbours (schoolteachers or whomever) observed bruising on Susie?

And so on. These same facts can be introduced through the parent or the parent's witnesses, but the above line of questioning minimizes the effect of the worker's testimony. If you want to push it, pose a final question to the worker:

> Q. So, to sum up, even though you saw the mother hit Susie once, it was on one occasion only, and she has no criminal record, no bruises were observed by her teacher, etc. (repeating all the matters that she has confirmed in response to the above questions).

The above template is the basic way in which a lawyer waters down facts that are against the parent. Does it work in practice? Rarely in protection matters. But maybe it tells the judge you are working your butt off to have your child returned.

Cross-examining the Agency worker

Evidence introduced at a protection trial rarely comes as a surprise. Before the trial, review the affidavit material and the pleadings, and you will probably have a good sense of exactly what the worker, and probably every other witness, will say and the things that will hurt you in the eyes of the court. You should have worked these issues to death in preparing your trial strategy. The court will likely view the Agency worker's evidence as "objective," even though, in many cases, an adversarial relationship has developed between you and the worker, so that objectivity may not exist in fact. But it will still exist in the eyes of most judges, and you should keep this in mind in cross-examination. The appearance of venting on the worker (as in trying to beat him or her up on the witness stand) only serves to hurt your cause—even though it would feel so damn good!

Personal knowledge of the worker

Unless the court has qualified the worker as an expert, he or she may testify only with respect to matters within his or her personal knowledge, such as things the worker saw or heard, so the first way to challenge a worker's testimony comes when the worker gives his or her evidence *in chief*; that is, when the Society lawyer questions him or her. During this testimony, be prepared to challenge on this basis—and this really involves paying close attention to his or her answers. Most Agency files go back years and contain entries from all sorts of sources, including anonymous ones, and the Agency occasionally tries to introduce this history through the current worker who has no personal knowledge of many of the allegations. Therefore, you must challenge this evidence on cross-examination. If he or she testifies that so-and-so said such-and-such, object to the evidence as hearsay; force the worker to produce so-and-so to give testimony. Unless the evidence is in your favour, or very benign, you should object strenuously to any evidence being introduced by any witness (other than an expert opinion) unless it is within his or her *personal knowledge*. There may be argument on this point, but *do not consent* to evidence being placed in front of the court unless you have an opportunity to cross-examine the party whose evidence it actually is. The exception to this position may be where the Agency recital is a substantially true rendering of the facts. In such a case, it may be prudent to consent to the admission of this evidence, to avoid having a series of witnesses give evidence against you and to avoid the perception of being obstructionist. In short, a brief recital of evidence through the worker may be less damaging than a series of witnesses who implicitly trash you, one after the other. If the Agency is seeking a final order to place the child with them (depending upon the jurisdiction, this might be crown wardship, permanent guardianship, permanent custody or a permanent intervention order), one must question whether there is any downside to insisting that every witness, except for experts, testifies only to matters within his or her personal knowledge. Some of these potential witnesses may not be available, which may help you; some may remember things differently than in the file and some may be neutralized through cross-examination.

Cross-examining the expert witness: the assessor

If you require cross-examination of an expert witness or the worker to make your case at trial, this fact alone should serve as an alarm bell—you desperately need an experienced lawyer to get your child returned. Cross-examination of a layperson is challenging enough, but court-seasoned experts, including the worker, challenge the most experienced counsel.

The most common expert in a protection trial is the clinical psychologist—namely, the assessor who conducted the Parenting Capacity Assessment that didn't go so well for you.

With the possible exception of your worker, the assessor who prepared the Parenting Capacity Assessment bangs in as the most critical witness in a protection case. In many cases, if the assessor's evidence remains without contradiction, your chances of success diminish—really, really diminish. *This means the assessor's evidence must be discredited or neutralized to have your child returned.* In fact, in many cases you are just exercising damage control with this witness and at the same time laying the groundwork for evidence to be led through your witnesses. To overcome a bad assessment just through your own testimony or that of your witnesses is very difficult, so any points gained on the cross-examination of the assessor and any groundwork laid for your case in questioning the assessor is very important to your success at trial. It is extremely difficult for an experienced lawyer to gain much headway with this witness and virtually impossible for an unrepresented parent.

A note of caution: if a Parenting Capacity Assessment exists, it probably means you consented to it and consented to the choice of assessor. Thus it is probably too late to contest the assessor's credentials, his relationship with the Agency or how often he makes recommendations in accordance with Agency wishes—or to raise any suggestion that the assessor is in some way an inappropriate choice. That ship has already sailed.

The plain-speak report

If your chances of success at trial hinge upon a successful cross-examination of the assessor, the first rule of attack (perhaps after giving a brief prayer to your favourite deity) is to seek clarity of the terminology used in the Parenting Capacity Assessment—to clear up the bunkum phraseology. This presupposes that you have dissected the report before trial and understood it. This approach at trial suggests the following method:

> Q. *Dr. Bones, you used the term—. Would you please tell us what that means, in lay terms?*

If you feel comfortable with the terminology of the report and understand the issues raised by it, then proceed to have the witness explain the report, clause by clause, in lay terms.

A Parenting Capacity Assessment identifies problems in the parent-child relationship, usually, but not always, suggesting a lack of the parenting skills needed to raise a particular child. A special-needs child, or an extremely needy child obviously raises the skill level required to parent that child, a complicating factor. A reasonable assumption suggests that every justice somewhat understands the underlying principles of an Assessment; however, not every judge appreciates its nuances, including the technical jargon. You need to present those issues in lay terms to ensure that the judge understands how the issues directly affect your child and your ability to parent. Clarifying the terminology will jumpstart the process and form the first step in putting your case across.

> Q. You use the term—. Do I understand that
> to mean—?

By this time, if the following points have not been covered, they should be addressed:

- Who hired the assessor?
- Whom did he interview, how often and for what duration? (Obtain the exact number of hours taken to interview each person.)
- What kind of tests were administered? Who took the tests, and what do those tests measure?
- Were the wishes of the children considered? (This is appropriate for older children only.) How were their wishes ascertained?
- What were the facts in dispute, and how did the assessor resolve the differences?
- What were the parenting weaknesses? What were the parenting strengths?
- What other sources did the assessor use?

The Assessment sets out the external sources relied upon, but you should confirm that there are no sources or reports other than those indicated. Some of the reports relied on will be more relevant than others and may require questioning their authors.

> Q. Is it true that you read the report of Dr. Expert?

Produce the report of Dr. Expert and show it to the assessor (i.e., "Is this the report you refer to?") Make the report an exhibit if it is not already one (e.g., "Your Honour, I ask that this be made an exhibit"). Do this with all the documents or reports relied upon by the assessor.

Find out whether the assessor reviewed the Agency file.

> Q. Is it true you read the Agency file in this matter?

And so on.

> Q. Is it true you reviewed the reports of the foster mother, Jane?
> Q. Is it true you reviewed the reports of the parent's access to the child?

Keep this up until you have reviewed all the background sources (expressly used or implied) for the Assessment. Before trial, you should already have reviewed the background material, so you can quiz the assessor on inconsistencies. Keep on going—plough through all the material that the assessor relied upon. As well, identify all of the people interviewed by the assessor. You may question the assessor about instructions from the Agency or conversations with any of the people interviewed.

Showing the parent's side to the assessor

If there are matters of fact in dispute, at some point during the cross-examination you must confront the assessor with your version. So let's assume that there is something in the material that the assessor reviewed that was factually incorrect or misleading—say, a conviction of the father for assault contained in the criminal record in the Agency's file. An experienced lawyer would probably approach the situation as follows—although there are many roads to Rome, and the solution suggested here might be less than effective, because to some extent it telegraphs the issue to the assessor. In fact, some lawyers would lay the trap with far more circumspection:

> Q. You were provided with a criminal record for the father that noted there was a conviction for assault against the father.
>
> Q. Did you rely on this conviction in your assessment of the father?

Presumably an assessor who is courtroom-experienced will waffle on this sort of a question. (He may say, "It was only one factor and not a major factor.")

> Q. And if I suggested to you that the father was only acting in self-defence on that occasion . . .

So you've put your position to the assessor and should do so on any other perceived factual areas in dispute. The questioning proceeds, suggesting to the witness that you object to the influence of the conviction, while in fact, down the road, you might suggest to this witness and the court that the parent consented to the conviction for other reasons and that there was no physical assault.

In addition to disputing the issues raised in the Assessment, you will also bolster your case with your own evidence and that of other witnesses you call about those same matters. The above brief recital should bring home the point that an experienced lawyer in your corner will increase the odds of having your child returned to you.

Testing in the assessment

All Assessments use standard tests to assist in the Assessment, and the report itself identifies what those tests are. These tests vary somewhat but address the same basic issues: the needs of the children and the parent's ability to meet those needs. The testing that the assessor undertakes and sets out in the report often yields little help to the parent's case. The tests and the veracity and reliability are complicated, and in fact, it is the results that are important. If you want to criticize the methodology in serious fashion, you will need to have your own expert on board. The results are presented in black and white and can take on an air of cast-in-stone finality, but this not always the case. There will have been eight to ten tests administered by the assessor, and the results will be detailed and conclusions offered as a result of those tests. In brief, the tests are designed to measure the parent's intelligence, memory, abstract reasoning, language skills, math skills and personality. The results of these tests will only fatally handicap you if they are so low as to show an extremely low-functioning parent (the sort who needs brain surgery or an extremely good backup as part of their plan).

The other test usually employed, and holding far more importance, is the PSI. (PSI stands for Parenting Stress Index, but a colleague suggests it is also a rude Latin phrase.) The PSI is a neutral series of questions to assess the difficult child, parental distress and parent-child conflict. There may be other parenting instruments used to support this test, and those should be reviewed in detail as well. While the framework of the PSI is neutral, applying the results calls for some subjectivity, but normally it is hard to make points against the assessor on this basis. The same is true of the tests used generally—they are what they are. Scoring points against an experienced assessor remains very difficult.

Although the test results may be difficult to challenge, it is a parenting capacity assessment, and addressing the issues set out below and submitting the assessor to intelligent cross-examination on those issues may bear fruit. Some possible approaches to the various issues when questioning the assessor are set out below; their usefulness will depend on the circumstances.

Physical care of the child

> Q. Did you review the entire file of the Agency?
>
> Q. Did you find anything in that file to suggest the child would be at physical risk with this parent?

Or you might ask:

> Q. I show you the plan and draw your attention to the Plan of Care filed by Joe Parent. Do you have any reason to believe that this plan would not keep the child safe?

As noted previously, a good Plan of Care addresses the issues raised by the Society, so this is one more way of drawing the court's attention to your knowledge of the child and the issues at play.

Emotional care of the child

> Q. You suggest that the child would be at emotional risk if the child was placed with Joe Parent. The Plan of Care filed by Mr. Parent provided as follows . . . I show you the plan and draw your attention to . . .

This line of questioning draws the court's attention to the features of the plan of care that deal with the emotional needs of the child, hopefully leading to the conclusion that the parent's plan satisfies or at least addresses the concerns of the Agency on this issue.

When the parent-child bond is challenged in the Agency's initial material, the prudent course for a parent is to sign up for a course or counselling to address this issue. Securing evidence about these courses or assistance, when you bring out your witnesses, might swing the court into your camp. It is a given that you can produce evidence of this sort when you place your case before the court, including observations from family members in a position to have witnessed your relationship with the child. But any concessions you could wrestle from the assessor in this regard would also help you. Questions put to the assessor about notes from access visits may also reinforce your position:

> Q. *I am showing you a note from an access visit on January 10. I suggest to you that the observations of Ms. Worker suggest a bond between little Susie and her mother.*

Parenting attitude

Does the assessment criticize your attitude toward parenting? You may have completed courses prior to trial that address this issue, so you can outline these efforts when you take the witness stand, and perhaps you can call the course teacher as well. Mea culpas can work effectively for you when coupled with objective measures undertaken to address the problem. Attending those courses indicates an understanding of the problem and steps toward solving it. Your evidence can also demonstrate appropriate attitudes toward parenting and setting limits for the children, or whatever else has given rise to the litigation.

Acknowledging problems

By the time the trial rolls around, you should have a realistic grasp of the problems with your case, problems that the justice is likely to see. If any issues are murky or disputed, assume the court leans toward giving the doubt to the Agency (see "the curse of child-protection work" in Chapter 1). Problems in parenting skills or with special needs of the child should obviously be addressed in your testimony, but again, very often you need to set up these issues when you are cross-examining the assessor. In most situations, this is not a question of "destroying" the assessor in the stand but of obtaining minor concessions here and there that give credibility to your case.

Your feelings toward your child

When the assessor has identified your feelings toward the child as a problem, you must deal with this in personal testimony and indicate that the feelings have been addressed or that you can put those feelings aside when parenting your child. Nothing else will get the job done.

Relating to your child

The ability to empathize with a child is something that the assessment addresses, and if you are found wanting in this capacity, you will need to convince a perhaps sceptical court that you have seen the light. A simple denial of this allegation will not wash. A perfect understanding of your child is not necessary, but a willingness to put your child's needs ahead of your own is. Address this in detail in your testimony.

Parent's background

Rightly or wrongly, your background is in play. Would production of either the maternal or paternal grandparents alleviate this concern or only confirm the risk? Issues of parental conflict must be addressed, testimony reinforcing other evidence produced, and perhaps witnesses called to give evidence of programs attended or therapists pulled in to address the "new" you. A serious anger-management problem on the father's part, cloaking an abusive relationship, poses difficult problems for the couple whose plan involves the father still being in residence. Judges view anger-management diplomas with scepticism. Sitting through court-mandated courses certifies little, but taking the stand, addressing problems, and discussing therapeutic efforts head-on may. If the family was dysfunctional and this drove the protection proceedings, the courses obviously don't hurt the case, but testimony must convince a court that the family dynamics have changed or that the abusive spouse has made great strides toward solving the problems at issue.

The history of addressing issues

Too many parents wind up at trial having alienated the professionals involved with the family. Each professional involved with a child is a potential witness for you, if only to show that you take directions from these professionals and try to work with them. Matters proceeding to the trial stage often include a fractured relationship between the worker and the parents, so it becomes even more important to show a willingness to address the issues of your child and your family through the other professionals already involved with the family. A wide variety of orders is available to a court in any given situation, but if the child still shows significant needs at the time of the trial, a parent viewed as part of the solution is in a far better position than one who is not.

Using cross-examination to minimize damage

Where the evidence presented damages your case, one technique to deal with it is to isolate the incident, present it as atypical, minimize it in cross-examination, and then reinforce the idea through, say, the parent's testimony. A note of caution: a rule most lawyers follow is not to ask a question unless they already know the answer. So, suppose the worker attended at the home and noted bruises on the children; proceed with your questioning very carefully, and watch for every opportunity to withdraw before serious damage is done. On cross-examination of the Agency worker, you might avail yourself of the following strategy of using leading questions like

> Q. *Isn't it true that there have been no other reports about injuries to the child reported to the Agency?*
>
> Q. *Isn't it true that when you searched the criminal records of the parents that there were no convictions for assault, or any crime involving violence, against either parent?*
>
> Q *Isn't it true that the parents had an explanation for those bruises?*

And so on.

The cheap shot

Beware of taking a cheap shot at any witness—but especially at the worker. The truth is that the worker appears in court far more often than you do; perhaps he or she has appeared in front of this judge before and impressed the judge with his or her character or professionalism.

The golden rule in cross-examination

Every witness presents a unique challenge and requires a separate, distinct type of cross-examination. The ability to read the type of witness improves with experience and remains a prime reason people hunt out lawyers to represent them in the process. After each Agency witness, you have an opportunity to cross-examine that witness. The first rule is this: if the witness has done nothing to hurt your case (a separate issue from whether they have offended you), don't cross-examine, as you can only make it worse. Lawyers refer to a violation of this rule as "pissing evidence down the drain." The second rule is this: reread and apply the first rule, because even experienced trial lawyers violate this rule on occasion, often with disastrous results.

The Agency reply

After all of the parents' witnesses have given evidence, the Agency addresses any new issues raised by those witnesses. As before, you may cross-examine any witnesses on this subsequent evidence.

When you should take the stand

By way of comparison, in a high percentage of criminal trials, lawyers do not put their clients in the witness stand because they know that they will probably just convict themselves. The basic assumption is that they will throw the case into the trash bin with only a tiny bit of help from the prosecutor. But in a *criminal* case the burden remains on the prosecution to make its case. *Protection* cases are a different kettle of fish, even though the theory is similar. My experience is this: if there are serious allegations against you—allegations of abuse, serious neglect or of drug or alcohol addiction—your child will not be returned to you unless the judge is able to observe you in the witness stand, giving evidence. And if the judge does not form a positive impression of you, your parenting capabilities and your ability to keep your child safe, your child will go into care at the conclusion of the trial. To emphasize this point: when credible, serious allegations have been levied during a protection matter, a parent must almost always take the witness stand and refute those allegations. If the judge does not acquire a warm and fuzzy feeling about you and your capability to care for this child and keep him or her from risk, then your child will go into foster care. In practice, clear across Canada, you must provide the judge with this sort of comfort level before your child returns home.

Chapter 12

Strategies for Specific Situations

The visible issues on the table are, in one sense, the easiest to deal with. It is harder to deal with issues that may be present but unspoken. Some judges tolerate the occasional use of marijuana; some don't. Some accept alternate lifestyles, but some don't. While these issues often cut along generational lines, sometimes they defy cataloguing. When issues such as these come into play or are suspected to be in play, someone needs to take the stand and convey child-care competence. Winning protection cases is about taking away the judge's apprehension and giving him or her a comfort level.

Strategies for typical radar sightings

Allegations of drug use against either parent require that you enter a treatment program as soon as possible; submit to testing, and get those negative test results in-hand. Any suggestion from you that you can manage the problem on your own will be viewed as—and probably is—denial. The same program should kick into place when the pregnant mother or the baby tests positive for illegal substances.

A child born with injuries consistent with abuse is largely a medical problem involving expert evidence. People with money hire their own experts, but experts often don't work for cases that are being defended on a budget or at Legal Aid rates. Big universities with medical faculties have experts on staff who may agree to assist parents. Online searches can help to locate these people. The more complicated the medical facts, the more likely it is that the expert findings alone will determine the outcome. On a positive note, these experts do not owe their living to the Agency, unlike many assessors. On the downside, the legal principle of *res ipsa loquitur* ("the facts speak for themselves") applies, and you will be obligated to provide a reasonable explanation for those injuries. The same principle applies to the child found to have ingested drugs.

The mother who has lost children to the Agency before, or who has a long history of Agency involvement, must show personal growth, growth that demonstrates that the previous risk has been addressed. Some mothers change through maturity and time, but you need external proof of that fact. My advice to such a parent is this: pursue every possible parenting course or any course that addresses the past problem. Parents have recovered from a bad court case with the Society and succeeded subsequently—but not without a great deal of commitment and effort. Parents have also recovered from addiction problems to succeed with the Society as well, and this progress can be monitored objectively. The issues involved must not only be addressed in fact but be *seen* to be addressed, through the proper programs or counselling or anything that leaves a trail that can be introduced during the next round of court appearances.

When an abusive relationship is the problem, and the spouse has not been dumped, any subsequent contact with the law, such as a conviction or even a serious incident that did not involve a conviction, would be fatal. I suggest mothers who have been assaulted call the police if another assault occurs. And take all the courses the Agency suggests. There are many spouses who have been arrested once for assault and decided to mend their ways, but an anger-management course still looks good on them.

The special-needs child requires parents who accept those needs and work with community-service providers to address them. A single parent with a special-needs child must, above all else, get the worker on his or her side. If this matter goes to trial, your proposed plan of care comes under close scrutiny. Health-care professionals will usually help you craft such a plan, perhaps be involved in the execution of it and maybe serve as witnesses in court. Extended-family support counts as a bonus. When you have other children who are also demanding, seek out community or religious groups and incorporate them into your plan—but above all else, have the support of a professional skilled with the disability in question.

Chapter 13

The Endings

The endings of most protection trials are tragic. Parents most often lose their case, and the child slips into the less-than-perfect (some would say evil) foster-care system, so the child loses as well. While the parents have some sort of closure and the Agency moves on to the next protection matter, the challenges for the child have just begun. Most of the cases going to trial involve the Agency seeking to have the children placed with them on a permanent basis. If the Agency succeeds and the child is found to be in need of protection or intervention, evidence will be presented on disposition (i.e., what happens to the child). Among the issues at this point is whether the parents will have access to these wards, and if so, what sort of access? If the child is young and adoptable, the judge will order no access to the parents, so the Agency may adopt the child out. When the child is older and the parents' problems not too severe, a court might order access, but tragically, it does not do so often enough.

One of the quirks guaranteed to raise the ire of parents is this: when the Agency is seeking to show that the parents can't look after the child, the worker and perhaps others will be describing in detail their observations about how *bad* and *out of control* the child is. As noted, after a protection finding is made, the court will hear argument on disposition, usually whether the parent is to have access. The Agency gets to suck and blow at the same time. The Agency worker for their adoption group, called to give evidence at this point, will address adoptability, and he or she will likely only present sweetness and light in the same child. "Why, certainly this child will be adopted, Your Honour." In fact, of course, the child is undoubtedly heading for warehousing.

By way of minor mitigation, the line worker remains in an adversarial position often and sees the family under stress. The adoption worker, however, has a much more positive job by definition. The adoption worker deals mostly with babies or young children and tries to find them homes with well-adjusted people who desperately want a child. As a result, adoption workers, by comparison, are somewhat sunny by nature, and their evidence usually reflects this. But the suck-and-blow aspect still exists and remains somewhat offensive to parents.

Appeals

In most jurisdictions, parents need an error of law to have a new trial ordered. And having a new trial ordered is realistically the best that they can hope for on appeal, as appeal courts are reluctant to substitute their opinion for that of a trial judge. Errors in law rarely exist. Experienced judges possess full knowledge of the issues involved and take care to leave no grounds for appeal (known as *bullet-proofing* in the trade). To evaluate the chances of having a new trial ordered, you probably need a lawyer to review the matter.

Postscript

Special-needs children and children older than a certain age (say age 5 or 6 at the outside), rarely get adopted, and they wind up in the foster-care system—a system, as noted, that is far from perfect. What is needed is a heroic judge to grant the Agency a set period of time to shoot for adoption, and then, if the child is not adopted, to revisit the issue of access.

It is possible for the parent to revisit the issue of access in the future, to seek to have the terms of the order varied, but legal-aid systems do not cover this cost as a rule. If the parent can maintain a relationship with the child, or if the child was older when ordered into care, then the child will often return to establish a serious relationship with the parent when he or she reaches the age of maturity and leaves the system. This is a common experience, which really speaks to whether the system truly is about what is best for the child.

Appendix

Protection Grounds

Alberta

(2) For the purposes of this Act, a child is in need of intervention if there are reasonable and probable grounds to believe that the survival, security or development of the child is endangered because of any of the following:

(a) the child has been abandoned or lost;

(b) the guardian of the child is dead and the child has no other guardian;

(c) the child is neglected by the guardian;

(d) the child has been or there is substantial risk that the child will be physically injured or sexually abused by the guardian of the child;

(e) the guardian of the child is unable or unwilling to protect the child from physical injury or sexual abuse;

(f) the child has been emotionally injured by the guardian of the child;

(g) the guardian of the child is unable or unwilling to protect the child from emotional injury;

(h) the guardian of the child has subjected the child to or is unable or unwilling to protect the child from cruel and unusual treatment or punishment.

(i) repealed 2003 c 16 s3.

117

(2.1) For the purposes of subsection (2)(c), a child is neglected if the guardian

    (a)   is unable or unwilling to provide the child with the necessities of life.

    (b)   is unable or unwilling to obtain for the child, or to permit the child to receive, essential medical, surgical or other remedial treatment that is necessary for the health or wellbeing of the child, or

    (c)   is unable or unwilling to provide the child with adequate care or supervision.

(3)   For the purposes of this Act,

    (a)   a child is emotionally injured

        (i)   if there is impairment of the child's mental or emotional functioning or development, and

        (ii)   if there is reasonable and probably grounds to believe that the emotional injury is the result of

            (A)   rejection

                (A.1) emotional, social, cognitive or physiological neglect,

            (B)   deprivation of affection or cognitive stimulation,

            (C)   exposure to domestic violence or severe domestic disharmony,

            (D)   inappropriate criticism, threats, humiliation, accusations or expectations of or toward the child,

            (E)   the mental or emotional condition of the guardian of the child or of anyone living in the same residence as the child;

            (F)   chronic alcohol or drug abuse by the guardian or by anyone living in the same residence as the child;

    (b)   a child is physically injured if there is substantial and observable injury to any part of the child's body as a result of the non-accidental application of force or an agent to the child's body that is evidenced by a laceration, a contusion, an abrasion, a scar, a fracture or other bony injury, a dislocation, a sprain, haemorrhaging, the rupture of viscous, a burn, a scald, frostbite, the loss or alteration of consciousness or physiological functioning or the loss of hair or teeth;

(c) a child is sexually abused if the child is inappropriately exposed or subjected to sexual contact, activity or behaviour including prostitution related activities.

British Columbia

13 (1) A child needs protection in the following circumstances:

(a) if the child has been, or is likely to be, physically harmed by the child's parent;

(b) if the child has been, or is likely to be, sexually abused or exploited by the child's parent;

(c) if the child has been, or is likely to be, physically harmed, sexually abused or sexually exploited by another person and if the child's parent is unwilling or unable to protect the child;

(d) if the child has been, or is likely to be, physically harmed because of neglect by the child's parent;

(e) if the child is emotionally harmed by the parent's conduct;

(f) if the child is deprived of necessary health care;

(g) if the child' development is likely to be seriously impaired by a treatable condition and the child's parent refuses to provide or consent to treatment;

(h) if the child's parent is unable or unwilling to care for the child and has not made adequate provision for the child's care;

(i) if the child is or has been absent from home in circumstances that endanger the child's safety or wellbeing;

(j) if the child's parent is dead and adequate provision has not been made for the child's care;

(k) if the child has been abandoned and adequate provision has not been made for the child's care;

(l) if the child is in the care of a director or another person by agreement and the child's parent is unwilling or unable to resume care when the agreement is no longer is force.

(1.1) For the purpose of subjection (1) (b) and (c) and section 14(1) (a) but without limiting the meaning of "sexually abused" or "sexually exploited", a child has been or is likely to be sexually abused or sexually exploited if the child has been, or is likely to be,

(a) encouraged or helped to engage in prostitution, or

(b) coerced or inveigled into engaging in prostitution.

(2) For the purpose of subsection (1) (e), a child is emotionally harmed if the child demonstrated severe

(a) anxiety,

(b) depression,

(c) withdrawal, or

(d) self-destructive or aggressive behaviour.

Manitoba

17(1) For purposes of the Act, a child is in need of protection where the life, health or emotional wellbeing of the child is endangered by the act or omission of a person.

17(2) Without restricting the generality of subsection (1), a child is in need of protection where the child

(a) is without adequate care, supervision or control;

(b) is in the care, custody, control or charge of a person

      (i)   who is unable or unwilling to provide adequate care, supervision or control of the child, or

      (ii)   who conduct endangers or might endanger the life, health or emotional wellbeing of the child, or

      (iii) who neglects or refuses to provide or obtain proper medical or other remedial care or treatment necessary for the health or wellbeing of the child or who refuses to permit such care or treatment to be provided to the child when the care or treatment is recommend by a duly qualified medical practitioner;

(c)   is abused or is in danger of being abused, including where the child is likely to suffer harm or injury due to child pornography;

(d)   is beyond the control of a person who has the care, custody, control or charge of the child;

(e)   is likely to suffer harm or injury due to behaviour, condition, domestic environment or associations of the child or of a person having care, custody, control or charge of the child;

(f)   is subjected to aggression or sexual harassment that endangers the life, health or emotional wellbeing of the child;

(g)   being under the age of 12 years, is left unattended and without reasonable provision being made for the supervision and safety of the child; or

(h)   is the subject, or is about to become the subject, of an unlawful adoption under The Adoption Act or of a sale under section 84.

New Brunswick

31(1) The security or development of a child may be in danger when

(a)   the child is without adequate care, supervision or control;

(b)   the child is living in unfit or improper circumstances;

(c)   the child is in the care of a person whose conduct endangers the life, health or emotional wellbeing or the child;

(d)   the child is in the care of a person whose conduct endangers the life, health or emotional wellbeing of the child;

(e)   the child is physically or sexually abused, physically neglected, sexually exploited or in danger of such treatment;

(f)   the child is living in a situation where there is domestic violence;

(g)   the child is in the care of a person who neglects or refuses to provide or obtain proper medical, surgical or other remedial care or treatment necessary for the health or wellbeing of the child or refuses to permit such care or treatment to be supplied to the child;

(h)   the child is beyond the control of the person caring for him;

(i)   the child by his behaviour, condition, environment or association, is likely to injure himself or others;

(j)   the child is in the care of a person who does not have a right to custody of the child, without the consent of a person having such right;

(k)   the child is in the care of a person who neglects or refuses to ensure that the child attends school; or

(l)   the child has committed an offence or, if the child is under the age of twelve years, has committed an act or omission that would constitutes an offence for which the child could be convicted if the child were twelve years of age or older.

Newfoundland

14. A child is in need of protective intervention where the child

    (a) is, or is at risk of being, physically harmed by the action or lack or appropriate action by the child's parent;

    (b) is, or is at risk of being, sexually abused or exploited by the child's parent;

    (c) is emotionally harmed by the parent's conduct;

    (d) is, or is at risk of being physically harmed by a person and the child's parent does not protect the child;

    (e) is, or is at risk of being, sexually abused or exploited by a person and the child's parent does not protect the child;

    (f) is being emotionally harmed by a person and the child's parent does not protect the child;

    (g) is in the custody of a parent who refuses or fails to obtain or permit essential medical, psychiatric, surgical or remedial care or treatment to be given to the child when recommended by a qualified health practitioner;

    (h) is abandoned;

    (i) has no living parent or a parent is unavailable to care for the child and has not made adequate provision for the child's care;

    (j) is living in a situation where there is violence; or

    (k) is actually or apparently under 12 years of age and has

        (i) been left without adequate supervision,

        (ii) allegedly killed or seriously injured another person or has caused serious damage to another person's property, or

        (iii) on more than one occasion caused injury to another person or other living thing or threatened either with or without weapons, to cause injury to another person or other living thing, either with the parent's encouragement or because the parent does not respond adequately to the situation.

Northwest Territories

7 (1) In this section, "parent" includes
- (a) a person who has lawful custody of a child other than the Director; and
- (b) except in paragraph (3)(q), a person having charge of a child.
- (2) Subsection (3) shall be interpreted
  - (a) with a recognition that differing cultural values and practices must be respected; and
  - (b) in accordance with community standards.
- (3) A child needs protection where
  - (a) the child has suffered physical harm inflicted by the child's parent or caused by the parent's inability to care and provide for or supervise and protect the child adequately;
  - (b) there is a substantial risk that the child will suffer physical harm inflicted by the child's parent or caused by the parent's inability to care and provide for or supervise and protect the child adequately;
  - (c) the child has been sexually molested or sexually exploited by the child's parent or by another person in circumstances where the child's parent knew or should have known of the possibility of sexual molestation or sexual exploitation and was unwilling or unable to protect the child;
  - (d) there is a substantial risk that the child will be sexually molested or exploited by the child's parent or by another person in circumstances where the child's parent knows or should know of the possibility of sexual molestation or sexual exploitation and is unwilling or unable to protect the child;

(e) the child has demonstrated severe anxiety, depression, withdrawal, self-destructive behaviour, or aggressive behaviour towards others; or any other severe behaviour that is consistent with the child having suffered emotional harm and the child's parent does not provide, or refuses or is unavailable or unable to consent to the provision of, services, treatment or healing processes to remedy or alleviate the harm;

(f) there is substantial risk that the child will suffer emotional harm of the kind described in paragraph (e), and the child's parent does not provide, or refuses or is unavailable or unable to consent to the provision of, services, treatment or healing to prevent the harm;

(g) the child suffers from a mental, emotional or developmental condition that, if not remedied, could seriously impair the child's development, and the child's parent does not provide, or refuses or is unavailable or unable to consent to the provision of, services, treatment or healing processes to remedy or alleviate the condition;

(h) the child has been subject to a pattern of neglect that has resulted in physical or emotional harm to the child;

(i) the child has been subject to a pattern of neglect and there is substantial risk that the pattern of neglect will result in physical or emotional harm to the child;

(j) the child has suffered physical or emotional harm caused by being exposed to repeated domestic violence by or towards a parent of the child and the child's parent fails to refuses to obtain services, treatment or healing processes to remedy or alleviate the harm;

(k) the child has been exposed to repeated domestic violence by or towards a parent of the child and there is a substantial risk that the exposure will result in physical or emotional harm to the child and the child's parent fails or refuses to obtain services, treatment or healing processes to prevent the harm;

(l)   the child's health or emotional or mental wellbeing has been harmed by the child's use of alcohol, drugs, solvents or similar substances, and the child's parent does not provide, or refuses or is unavailable or unable to consent to the provision of, services, treatment or healing processes to remedy or alleviate the harm;

(m)   there is a substantial risk that the child's health or emotional or mental wellbeing will be harmed by the child's use of alcohol, drugs, solvents or similar substances, and the child's parent does not provide, or refuses or is unavailable or unable to consent to the provision of, services, treatment or healing processes to prevent the harm;

(n)   the child requires medical treatment to cure, prevent or alleviate serious physical harm or serious physical suffering, and the child's parent does not provide, or refuses or in unavailable or unable to consent to the provision of, the treatment;

(o)   the child suffers from malnutrition of a degree that, if not immediately remedied could seriously impair the child's growth or development or result in permanent injury or death;

(p)   the child has been abandoned by the child's parent without the child's parent having made adequate provision for the child's care or custody and the child's extended family has not made adequate provision for the child's care or custody;

(q)   the child's parents have died without making adequate provision for the child's care or custody and the child's extended family has not made adequate provision for the child's care or custody;

(r)   the child's parent is unavailable or unable to unwilling to properly care for the child and the child's extended family has not made adequate provision for the child's care or custody; or

(s)   the child is less than 12 years of age and has killed or seriously injured another person or has persisted in injuring others or causing damage to the property of others, and services, treatment or healing processes are necessary to prevent a recurrence, and the child's parent does not provide, or refuses to, is unavailable or unable to consent to the provision of the services, treatment or healing process. S.N.W.T. 2002, c.14.

Nova Scotia

22(1) In this Section, "substantial risk" means a real chance of danger that is apparent on the evidence.

(2)   A child is in need of protective services where

(a)   the child has suffered physical harm, inflicted by a parent or guardian of the child or caused by the failure of a parent or guardian to supervise and protect the child adequately;

(b)   there is a substantial risk that the child will suffer physical harm inflicted or cause as described in clause (a);

(c)   the child has been sexually abused by a parent or guardian of the child, or by another person where a parent or guardian of the child knows or should know of the possibility of sexual abuse and fails to protect the child;

(d)   there is a substantial risk that the child will be sexually abused as described in clause (c);

(e)   a child requires medical treatment to cure, prevent or alleviate physical harm or suffering, and the child's parent or guardian does not provide, or refuses or is unavailable or is unable to consent to, the treatment;

(f) the child has suffered emotional harm, demonstrated by severe anxiety, depression, withdrawal, or self-destructive or aggressive behaviour and the child's parent or guardian does not provide, or refuses or is unavailable or unable to consent to, services or treatment to remedy or alleviate the harm;

(g) there is a substantial risk that the child will suffer emotional harm of the kind described in clause (f), and the parent or guardian does not provide, or refuses or is unavailable or unable to consent to, services or treatment to remedy or alleviate the harm;

(h) the child suffers from a mental, emotional or developmental condition that, if not remedied, could seriously impair the child's development and the child's parent or guardian does not provide, or refuses or is unavailable or unable to consent to, services or treatment to remedy or alleviate the condition;

(i) the child has suffered physical or emotional harm caused by being exposed to repeated domestic violence by or towards a parent or guardian of the child, and the child's parent or guardian fails or refuses to obtain services or treatment to remedy or alleviate the violence;

(j) the child has suffered physical harm caused by chronic and serious neglect by a parent or guardian of the child, and the parent or guardian does not provide, or refuses or is unavailable or unable to consent to, services or treatment to remedy or alleviate the harm;

(ja) there is a substantial risk that the child will suffer physical harm inflicted or caused as described in clause (j);

(k) the child has been abandoned, the child's only parent or guardian has died or is unavailable to exercise custodial rights over the child and has not made adequate provisions for the child's care and custody, or the child is in the care of an agency or another person and the parent or guardian of the child refuses or is unable or unwilling to resume the child's care and custody;

(l) the child is under twelve years of age and has killed or seriously injured another person or caused serious damage to another person's property, and services or treatment are necessary to prevent a recurrence and a parent or guardian of the child does not provide, or refuses or is unavailable or unable to consent to, the necessary services or treatment;

(m) the child is under twelve years of age and has on more than one occasion injured another person or caused loss or damage to another person's property, with the encouragement of a parent or guardian of the child or because of the parent or guardian's failure to inability to supervise the child adequately, 1990, c.5, s. 22; 1996.

Ontario

(2) A child is in need of protection where,

(a) the child has suffered physical harm, inflicted by the person having charge of the child or caused by or resulting from that person's,

  (i) failure to adequately care for, provide form supervise or protect the child, or

  (ii) pattern of neglect in caring for, providing for, supervising or protecting the child;

(b) there is a risk that the child is likely to suffer physical harm inflicted by the person having charge of the child or caused by or resulting from that person's,

  (i) failure to adequately care for, provide for, supervise or protect the child, or

  (ii) pattern of neglect in caring for, proving for, supervising or protecting the child;

(c)   the child has been sexually molested or sexually exploited, by the person having charge of the child or by another person where the person having charge of the child knows or should know of the possibility of sexual molestation or sexual exploitation and fails to protect the child;

NOTE: On a day to be named by proclamation of the Lieutenant Governor, clause (c) is repealed by the Statutes of Ontario, 2008, chapter 21, section 2 and the following substituted:

'c.   the child has been sexually molested or sexually exploited, including by child pornography, by the person having charge of the child or by another person where the person having charge of the child knows of the possibility of sexual molestation or sexual exploitation and fails to protect the child'; See: 2008, c. 21, ss. 2, 6.

(d)   there is a risk that the child is likely to be sexually molested or sexually exploited as described in clause (c);

(e)   the child requires medical treatment to cure, prevent or alleviate physical harm or suffering and the child's parent or the person having charge of the child does not provide, or refuses or is unavailable or unable to consent to, the treatment;

(f)   the child has suffered emotional harm, demonstrated by serious
    (i)   anxiety,
    (ii)   depression,
    (iii)   withdrawal,
    (iv)   self-destructive or aggressive behaviour, or delayed development,

(v) delayed development, and there are reasonable grounds to believe that the emotional harm suffered by the child results from the actions, failure to act or pattern of neglect on the part of the child's parent or the person having charge of the child;

(f.1) the child has suffered emotional harm of the kind described in subclause (f) (i), (ii), (iii), (iv) or (v) and the child's parent or the person having charge of the child does not provide, or refuses or is unavailable or unable to consent to, services or treatment to remedy or alleviate the harm;

(g) there is a risk that the child is likely to suffer emotional harm of the kind described in subclause (f) (i), (ii), (iii), (iv) or (v) resulting from the actions, failure to act or pattern of neglect on the part of the child's parent or the person having charge of the child;

(g.1) there is a risk that the child is likely to suffer emotional harm of the kind described in sub clause (f) (i), (ii), (iii), (iv), or (v) and that the child's parent or the person having charge of the child does not provide, or refuses or is unavailable or unable to consent to, services or treatment to prevent the harm;

(h) the child suffers from a mental, emotional or developmental condition that, if not remedied, could seriously impair the child's development and the child's parent or the person having charge of the child does not provide, or refuses or is unavailable or unable to consent to, treatment to remedy or alleviate the condition;

(i) the child has been abandoned, the child's parent has died or is unavailable to exercise his or her custodial rights over the child and has not made adequate provision for the child's care and custody, or the child is in a residential placement and the parent refuses or is unable or unwilling to resume the child's care and custody;

(j) the child is less than twelve years old and has killed or seriously injured another person or caused serious damage to another person's property, services or treatment are necessary to prevent a recurrence and the child's parent or the person having charge of the child does not provide, or refuses or is unavailable or unable to consent to, those services or treatment.

(k) the child is less than twelve years old and has on more than one occasion injured another person or caused loss or damage to another person's property, with the encouragement of the person having charge of the child or because of that person's failure or inability to supervise the child adequately; or

(l) the child's parent is unable to care for the child and the child is brought before the court with the parent's consent and, where the child is twelve years of age or older, with the child's consent, to be dealt with under this Part. R.S.O. 1990, c. C.11, s. 37 (2); 1999, c. 2, s 9.

Prince Edward Island

3. A child is in need of protection where
   (a) the child has suffered physical harm inflicted by a parent;
   (b) the child has suffered harm caused by
      (i) neglect of the child by a parent.
      (ii) failure of a parent to adequately supervise or protect the child, or
      (iii) failure of a parent to provide for the adequate supervision or protection of the child;

(c)   the child has been sexually abused by a parent or by another person where the parent knew or ought to have known of the possibility of sexual abuse of the child and the parent failed to protect the child;

(d)   the child has been harmed as a result of being sexually exploited for the purposes of prostitution and the parent has failed or been unable to protect the child;

(e)   the child has suffered emotional harm inflicted by a parent, or by another person, where the parent knew or ought to have known that the other person was emotionally abusing the child and the parent failed to protect the child;

(f)   the child has suffered physical or emotional harm caused by being exposed to domestic violence by or towards a parent;

(g)   the child is at substantial risk of suffering harm within the meaning of clause (a), (b), (c),(d), (e), or (f);

(h)   the child requires specific medical, psychological or psychiatric treatment to cure, prevent or ameliorate the effects of a physical or emotional condition or harm suffered, and the parent does not, or refuses to obtain treatment or is unavailable or unable to consent to treatment;

(i)   the child suffered from a mental, emotional or developmental condition, that, if not addresses, could seriously harm the child and the parent does not or refuses to obtain treatment or is unavailable or unable to consent to services or treatment to remedy or ameliorate the effects of the condition;

(j)   the child has been abandoned, or the only parent of the child has died or is unavailable to take custody of the child, and adequate provisions have not been made for the care of the child;

(k)   the child is in the custody of the Director or another person and the parent of the child refuses or in unable to resume custody of the child;

(l) the child is less than 12 years old, and the child, in the opinion of the Director,

    (i) may have killed or seriously injured another person,

    (ii) poses a serious danger to another person, or

    (iii) may have caused significant loss or damage to property, and the parent of the child does not obtain or is unwilling to consent to treatment for the child which may be necessary to prevent a recurrence of the incident or danger; or

(m) the past parenting by the parent has put a child at significant risk of harm within the meaning of this section. 2000 (2nd), c. 3, s.3.

Quebec

38. (1) For the purposes of this Act, the security or development of a child is considered to be in danger where

(a) his parents are deceased or do not, in fact, assume responsibility for his care, maintenance or education;

(b) his mental or affective development is threatened by the lack of appropriate care or by the isolation in which he is maintained or by serious and continuous emotional rejection by his parents;

(c) his physical health is threatened by the lack of appropriate care;

(d) he is deprived of the material conditions of life appropriate to his needs and to the resources of his parents or of the persons having custody of him;

(e) he is in the custody of a person whose behaviour or way of life creates a risk of moral or physical danger for the child;

(f)   he is forced or induced to beg, to do work disproportionate to his capacity or to perform for the public in a manner that is unacceptable for his age;

(g)   he is the victim of sexual abuse or he is subject to physical ill-treatment through violence or neglect;

(h)   he has serious behavioural disturbances and his parents fail to take the measures necessary to put an end to the situation in which the development or security of their child is in danger or the remedial measures taken by them fail.

Security or development not endangered

(2)   however, the security of development of a child whose parents are deceased is not considered to be in danger if a person standing *in loco parentis* has, in fact, assumed responsibility for the child's care, maintenance and education, taking the child's needs into account. 1981, c. 2, s. 8; 1984, c. 4, s. 18; 1994, c. 35, s. 23

Security or development endangered

38.1 The security or development of a child may be considered to be in danger where

(a)   he leaves his own home, a foster family, a facility maintained by an institution operating a rehabilitation centre or a hospital centre without authorization while his situation is not under the responsibility of the director of youth protection;

(b)   he is of school age and does not attend school, or is frequently absent without reason;

(c)   his parents do not carry out their obligations to provide him with care, maintenance and education or do not exercise stable supervision over him, while he has been entrusted to the care of an institution or foster family for one year. 1984, c. 4, s. 18; 1989, c. 53, s. 4; 1992, c. 21, ss. 221, 345; 1994, c. 35, s. 24

Saskatchewan

11. A child is in need or protection where:
    (a)   as a result of action or omission by the child's parent:
        (i)   the child has suffered or is likely to suffer physical harm;
        (ii)   the child has suffered or is likely to suffer a serious impairment of mental or emotional functioning;
        (iii)   the child has been or is likely to be exposed to harmful interaction for a sexual purpose, including involvement in prostitution and including conduct that may amount to an offence within the meaning of the Criminal Code;
        (iv)   medical, surgical or other recognized remedial care or treatment that is considered essential by a duly qualified medical practitioner has not been or is not likely to be provided to the child;
        (v)   the child's development is likely to be seriously impaired by failure to remedy a mental, emotional or developmental condition; or
        (vi)   the child has been exposed to domestic violence or severe domestic disharmony that is likely to result in physical or emotional harm to the child;
    (b)   there is no adult person who is able and willing to provide for the child's needs, and physical or emotional harm to the child has occurred or is likely to occur; or
    (c)   the child is less than 12 years of age and:

        (i)   there is reasonable and probable grounds to believe that:

             (A)   the child has committed an act that, if the child were 12 years of age or more, would constitute an offence under the Criminal Code, the Narcotic Control Act (Canada) or Part III or Part IV of the Food and Drug Act (Canada); and

             (B)   family services are necessary to prevent a recurrence; and

        (ii)   the child's parent is unable or unwilling to provide for the child's needs.

Yukon

21(1) A child is in need of protective intervention if the child

    (a)   is, or is likely to be, physically harmed by the child's parent;

    (b)   is, or is likely to be, sexually abused or exploited by the child's parent;

    (c)   is, or is likely to be, emotionally harmed by the conduct of the child's parent;

    (d)   is, or is likely to be, physically harmed by a person and the child's parent does not protect the child;

    (e)   is, or is likely to be, sexually abused or exploited by a person and the child's parent does not protect the child;

    (f)   is, or is likely to be, emotionally harmed by a person's conduct and the child's parent does not protect the child;

    (g)   is being deprived of health care that, in the opinion of a health care provider, is necessary to preserve the child's life, prevent imminent serious physical or mental harm, or alleviate severe pain;

    (h)   is abandoned;

(i) has no living parent or no parent is available to care for the child and adequate provision for the child's care has been made; or

(j) is under 12 years of age and has

(i) allegedly killed or caused serious injury to another person, or

(ii) on more than one occasion caused injury to another person or threatened, either with or without weapons, to cause injury to another person, either with the parent's encouragement or because the parent does not respond adequately to the situation, and the parent of the child does not provide services or treatment aimed at preventing a recurrence, or is unavailable or unable to consent to the services or treatment.

(2) For the purpose of paragraphs (1) (b) and (e), but without limiting the meaning of "sexually abused or exploited", a child has been or is likely to be sexually abused or exploited if the child has been or is likely to be

(a) inappropriately exposed or subjected to sexual contact, activity or behaviour, including prostitution related activities; or

(b) encouraged or counselled to engage in prostitution.

(3) For the purpose of paragraphs (1) (c) and (f), but without limiting the meaning of "emotionally harmed", a child has been, or is likely to be, emotionally harmed by the conduct of a parent or other person if the parent or other person demonstrates a pattern of behaviour that is detrimental to the child's emotional or psychological wellbeing.

About the author

Allan Dare Pearce, "Dare" to friends and colleagues, was awarded a B. A. and LL.B. degree from the University of Windsor. He attended on a Department of Justice fellowship at the University of Ottawa where he received a post-graduate diploma in legislative drafting. He was subsequently awarded an LL.M. degree from Leicester University.

Mr. Pearce was called to the bar of Ontario and is a member in good standing with the Law Society of Upper Canada.

He was formerly a member of the Law Society of the Northwest Territories and formerly Chief Legislative Counsel for the Government of the Northwest Territories.

Mr. Pearce was formerly a counsel with the Privy Council Office Section of the Department of Justice.

Mr. Pearce currently practises law in Windsor, Ontario with the law firm of Pearce Ducharme Family Law.

He edited *Revised Regulations of the Northwest Territories, 1980*, a 1679 page volume of the consolidated regulations of the Northwest Territories.

Mr. Pearce authored *Some Practical Guidelines for Incorporating Codes Into Legislation, The Canadian Bar Review, December of 1982*.

He is the author of a work of fiction, *Paris in April*, available in most e-book formats.